D0217504

Foster Carers

Supporting Parents

Series edited by David Quinton, Professor of Psychosocial Development, University of Bristol

Consultant editors: Carolyn Davies and Caroline Thomas, Department for Education and Skills and Department of Health

This important series is the result of an extensive government-funded research initiative into how we can best support parents and carers as part of an integrated service for children. Underpinning current policy directives including the Children's National Service Framework, the titles in the series are essential reading for practitioners, policy makers and academics working in child care.

Foster Carers

Why They Stay and Why They Leave

Ian Sinclair, Ian Gibbs and Kate Wilson

Jessica Kingsley Publishers
London and New York

First published in the United Kingdom in 2004
by Jessica Kingsley Publishers Ltd
116 Pentonville Road
London N1 9JB, England
and
29 West 35th Street, 10th fl.
New York, NY 10001-2299, USA

www.jkp.com

Copyright © 2004 Ian Sinclair, Ian Gibbs and Kate Wilson

Library of Congress Cataloging in Publication Data
Sinclair, Ian, 1938-
  Foster carers : why they stay and why they leave / Ian Sinclair, Ian Gibbs, and Kate Wilson. --
1st American pbk. ed.
      p. cm.
  Includes bibliographical references and index.
  ISBN 1-84310-172-6 (pbk.)
  1. Foster home care--Great Britain. 2. Foster parents--Great Britain. I. Gibbs, Ian. II. Wilson,
Kate, 1943- III. Title.
HV887.G5S56 2004
362.73'3'0941--dc22

                                                                              2004001077

British Library Cataloguing in Publication Data
A CIP catalogue record for this book is available from the British Library
ISBN 1 84310 172 6

Printed and Bound in Great Britain by
Athenaeum Press, Gateshead, Tyne and Wear

Contents

Acknowledgements

As always this has been a team effort. Our work in preparing the book has been greatly aided by the efforts of Helen Jacobs, Erin Bell and Claire Baker.

Throughout the project we have benefited from the wise counsel of an advisory group composed of Professor Jane Aldgate, Jane Allberry, Dr Carolyn Davies, Helen Jones, Gerri McAndrew, Professor David Quinton, Caroline Thomas and Professor John Triseliotis.

Our thanks must also go to those who, for reasons of confidentiality, we cannot name: the managers and liaison officers in the seven local authorities who were prepared to participate in, and support, a project that made great demands on their time, especially in completing the Census of Registered Foster Carers at two points in time.

Our main thanks are reserved for the 940 or so foster carers who responded to our General Questionnaire on which much of this book is based. We hope this book does both justice to their concerns and reflects our admiration for the work they do.

Ian Sinclair
Ian Gibbs
Kate Wilson

Chapter One

Background and Introduction

Introduction

Foster care is a remarkable and paradoxically a very ordinary activity. It involves children and young people living and being cared for in 'ordinary families'. These families, however, are not their own but are sponsored, funded and regulated by the state. In England as elsewhere the linchpin of this system is the 25,000 or so foster carers who undertake the awesome task of looking after other people's children. This book is about them.

The book is written at a time of concern about the shortage of foster carers, a growing acknowledgement of the complexity of the task and a recognition that if we are to recruit and keep foster carers in sufficient numbers then effort must be put into this both nationally and locally. To do this successfully, we need to know more about the strengths and strains of the current system: who the carers are and who they are not; what they expect from fostering and what rewards they get from it; what they find difficult about it; and why they continue to foster or cease doing so. Our research was designed to contribute to an understanding of these issues and thus to underpin efforts to reduce strain and decrease turnover. We hope that it will be useful to all those involved in foster care, whether carers themselves, social workers, managers or policy makers and thus, indirectly, to foster children themselves.

The book is one of a set of three complementary titles that draw on the findings of three linked studies of foster care undertaken over a six-year period in seven English local authorities. Each book explores a different aspect of fostering. As already described this, the first book, concentrates primarily on foster carers: who they are, what diminishes or increases the stresses they feel and what makes them likely to find foster care fulfilling and to want to continue. The second book focuses by and large on foster placements, the children in them and what makes the placements go well or badly. The third looks at how these same children were doing after three years, and what might explain what has happened to them. Although they form a set, they will appeal differently to different readers, and each book can be read on its own. Taken as a complete study, they provide, we hope, a unique portrait of foster care on the cusp of the twentieth and twenty-first centuries.

Background to the study

Our primary reason for studying foster care was simply its intrinsic importance. Most children and young people who are cared for by local authorities live in foster families. On the most recent figures for England around 60,000 children are officially looked after in the care system at any one time (Department of Health 2003). Two-thirds of these are fostered.

Many of these looked-after children (for ease of reading we shall usually refer to children rather than children and young people, except when the distinction is important) have spent a considerable time in foster care. The latest statistical report does not give details of their lengths of stay. However, a relatively recent return shows that eight out of ten had been in the care system for at least a year and nearly a quarter had been looked after continuously for five years or more. Others enter briefly and return home or oscillate between home and fostering. So foster care is marked not only by the onerous responsibility of providing long-term family care for children but also by much coming and going. Overall around 82,000 children are at some stage looked after over the course of a year (Department of Health 2003).

During the 1980s and 1990s foster care more or less continuously increased its 'market share' of children who are looked after by local authorities (see, for example, Berridge 1997). This trend reflected its perceived superiority over residential care as a form of provision that is cheaper, less institutional and less apparently prone to scandal. In keeping with its organisational success there was little perceived need to carry out research upon it. In the 1990s the major Department of Health research initiative on looked-after children concentrated on the scandal-prone and high-profile residential sector rather than the numerically much larger number of children in foster care (Utting 1997).

Yet despite its apparent success foster care contained within it a number of tensions. At least seven major trends were involved (for what follows see also

Berridge 1997; House of Commons Health Committee 1998; Triseliotis, Borland and Hill 2000).

1.   The population of foster care has been changing. Young children are rarely placed with foster carers without attempts at rehabilitation. This combined with the reduction in residential care has probably led to a more difficult clientele, including a higher proportion who enter foster care as teenagers or after they have been disturbed by repeated 'failures' at home. The proportion of those entering the care system that have had previous experience of it seems to have been rising (Packman and Hall 1998) while the length of time they spend in the system has been increasing. Both trends suggest that their difficulties at home are even greater than before (Department of Health 2003).

2.   There has been a change in the overall role of foster carers. Studies in the 1970s emphasised the degree to which foster carers then saw themselves not as temporary carers, but as parents who at best were likely to permit contact between birth parents and children 'on sufferance' (Adamson 1973; George 1970). By contrast the Children Act (1989) has emphasised the need for birth parents to play a continuing and involved role with foster children. This has reinforced the expectations of social workers and the aspirations of carers for a more professional status. No longer are carers expected to 'bring children up as their own'. Instead they are to share care with birth parents, avoid alienating their foster children's affections from their families of origin and treat as partners parents whom they might once have regarded as rivals or the sources of their foster children's ills.

3.   The combination of changes in role and in the problems presented by the children has not been accompanied by the development of a sophisticated theory of fostering. Special schemes have arisen to cope with difficult teenagers but they typically lack the elaborate theoretical justifications of their North American counterparts (Hill *et al.* 1999).

4.   The change in role has been accompanied by increasing attempts to professionalise fostering. This has been promoted by the growth of professional fostering schemes (Hazel 1981; Shaw and Hipgrave 1983, 1989) and is evidenced, for example, in the growth of a professional association (formerly the National Foster Care Association, now Fostering Network) and in debates about the role

of payment to foster carers rather than simply allowances notionally based on costs (Oldfield 1997).

5.   There have been continuing concerns about the performance of foster care: more specifically its difficulty in providing long-term stability, the extent and persistence of educational failure among foster children and the lack of effective aftercare for those who leave (Garnett 1992; Heath, Colton and Aldgate 1994; Jackson 1994, 2001; Stein 1997).

6.   There is considerable concern about the lack of choice when making foster care placements, the resulting danger that children may be placed in placements which would not naturally have been chosen, or even not placed at all, and the particularly acute shortage of placements for certain groups such as ethnic minorities and teenagers (Triseliotis *et al.* 2000; Waterhouse 1997).

7.   Local authorities, long the sole providers of foster care services, have been facing competition from the growth of independent foster care with resulting concerns about the impact of these services on costs and their ability to lure away the authorities' own foster carers (Sellick 1992).

This combination of problems has led some to conclude that foster care faces a crisis (National Foster Care Association 1997). Even researchers viewing the scene in different parts of the United Kingdom have detected a lack of coherent policy. Good intentions and attractive phrases abound but apparently they are not always translated into measurable targets or coherent policies over such issues as payments and allowances, training or fostering by relatives (Pithouse and Parry 1999; Triseliotis *et al.* 2000).

The most recent responses to these issues have been provided by the government's *Quality Protects* and then *Choice Protects* programmes, which among other things give high priority to increasing the number of foster carers, the stability of placements, the education and aftercare of children in the care system and the quality of the system for managing them. The programmes have been reinforced by a number of performance indicators against which departments are judged.

In general the programmes see an ability to choose between placements as central to the success of the 'looked-after system'. Choice implies an adequate number and variety of foster carers. This in turn implies a need to increase the numbers recruited or decrease the numbers leaving. An obvious way of doing this is to increase the attractiveness of foster caring by providing better support. This should reduce turnover. It may also increase recruitment. Many foster carers are recruited by existing foster carers who are not likely to put in a good word for a service where they are unhappy (Triseliotis *et al.* 2000). There is also some evidence that foster carers move from the local authority to the independent sector at least partly in the hope of better support (Sellick 1992, 2002).

There are, of course, other reasons for providing support. Professional support is a proper expectation of those undertaking a professional role. It should help to manage the tensions arising from more difficult children and a more ambiguous caring task. There is some evidence that appropriate and timely support might diminish the number of fostering breakdowns or disruptions. Berridge and Cleaver (1987), for example, found that an agency that appeared to manage and support its staff well had fewer placement breakdowns than expected. Some researchers (Aldgate and Hawley 1986; Quinton *et al.* 1998) emphasise the need for early supportive interventions to interrupt the negative spirals of difficult behaviour and carer rejection that lead to breakdown. As research in our second book will show there is certainly an association between carer stress and placement breakdown – a finding supported by Farmer and her colleagues' study of placements for teenagers (Farmer, Moyers and Lipscombe 2002).

In our view, however, the primary and overwhelming reason for providing support is a moral one. As we shall see foster care can be deeply satisfying to those who provide it. Most commonly it is. Nevertheless it can also be devastating. Foster carers invite others to share their home. In this way they make themselves vulnerable to accusations of abuse, to conflict with the families of their children, to late nights and confrontations, to the hassles of attending meetings and other bureaucratic events, to feelings of failure when things do not go well and to sadness when children whom they may have come to love move on. They do all this for, in most cases, expenses rather than pay and without arrangements for pensions. It is morally imperative to provide them with adequate support. The question our study had to examine is what kind of support was required.

Recent relevant studies

Many of the issues identified above were 'put on the map' by earlier research on foster care. Two large studies, spaced far apart (Bebbington and Miles 1990; Gray and Parr 1957), have described the characteristics of foster carers. Generally these have suggested that foster families tend to follow a rather traditional pattern. Foster families have tended to be based on white, married couples where the husband works while the wife works only part-time or not at all. These facts have raised concerns about the continuing supply of carers as more women work, the time given to raising children reduces, and divorce or separation increases the number of lone carers.

Other studies have confirmed the shortage of foster carers. This has been particularly acute in areas of high need for foster care (Bebbington and Miles 1990) and among those willing and suitable to take special groups such as adolescents, children from minority ethnic and sibling groups (Coffin 1993; Waterhouse 1997). There has been work on the need to recruit black carers for black children and the requirements for doing so successfully (Caesar, Parchment and Berridge 1994) and on the particular requirements of carers who are also relatives (Broad 2001a, 2001b). Other research has included the impact of fostering, particularly fostering breakdowns, on carers (Aldgate and Hawley 1986; Baxter 1989; Berridge and Cleaver 1987) or on the carers' children (Ames Reed 1993; Kaplan 1988; Part 1993; Pugh 1996).

Early work suggested that the shortage of carers was compounded by the frequency and rapidity with which carers left. Jones (1975) found that 40 per cent of a sample of those who stopped fostering had done so in the first year. This suggested that support might enhance retention, and American studies have examined the relevance of support to carers' intentions of leaving (Reindfleisch, Bean and Denby 1998; Rhodes, Orme and Buehler 2001). Some British studies have also considered carers' needs for support (Ramsay 1996; Sellick 1992). In general, carer dissatisfaction focuses particularly on inadequate information on foster children, poor support out of hours, lack of relief breaks, inadequate support from social workers, and inefficient handling of practical matters (e.g. repayment for costs of fostering – see Kirton 2001).

Despite its importance this earlier work has not included a large English systematic study of the kind of support carers need and the part this plays in enabling them to continue fostering. Recently, however, a major study (Triseliotis *et al.* 2000) has tackled these issues in a Scottish context. This Scottish study was conceived and begun before ours, is in many ways similar in design and size, and certainly anticipates many of the findings in this first book. We believe that part of the value of our book lies in confirming that the Scottish results largely hold south of the border and in a study carried out by different researchers using slightly different methods. Both books complement each other by covering ground that the other did not.

Two other recent studies are also particularly relevant. Farmer and her colleagues (2002), in an important study of teenage placements, have examined both the sources of stress among foster carers and the relationship between carer stress and outcomes. More recently Walker and her colleagues (2002) have examined a Scottish scheme for fostering teenagers who would otherwise have been in secure accommodation. Despite the difficult nature of this clientele none of the carers ceased fostering over the three years, a fact which suggests that the kind of support provided must have been particularly appropriate. In the course of the book we shall discuss the degree to which our own findings are supported by and also support this other research.

The study

The study was carried out in seven local authorities. These were selected to provide geographical and social variety and to include authorities with significant numbers from ethnic minorities. They included two London boroughs (one from inner and one from outer London), two shire counties, one new unitary authority (a sizeable city) and two metropolitan districts. We deal in Appendix 1 with the additional – and very important – preliminary questions about the degree to which the samples can be regarded as representative and the degree to which these authorities taken together can be regarded as representative of the situation in England as a whole. We point out there that compared with the national picture our sample does under-represent relative carers. With this possible exception, which affects discussion of this group, we do not think that any of the possible sources of bias is sufficiently serious to have a significant impact on our conclusions.

The research focused on all those registered as foster carers with these local authorities and combined quantitative and qualitative techniques.

We began by carrying out a census of all the foster carers in the seven areas. All the authorities had family placement or link social workers who were allocated to each foster family. We asked these workers to complete a brief, one-page pro-forma on each foster family. The questions asked whether the foster carer was working and other matters that might affect his or her readiness to respond to our questionnaires (see Appendix 2 for the pro-forma used).

The primary purpose of the census was to ensure that we could check for any bias that might distinguish those answering our questionnaires from those who did not. Nevertheless it also provided useful information on almost all the foster carers registered in the seven authorities. A follow-up 17 months later provided information on which ones continued to foster. This allowed us to estimate turnover. We were also able to compare carers who continued with those who did not. This helped us to understand the reasons for turnover.

In addition to the census at two points in time, our main source of information was a survey of all foster carers in the authorities. The General Questionnaire survey asked carers for information about themselves, the kind of foster caring in which they were involved and the support they received. We also asked about the impact of fostering on them and their family, their attitudes towards it, their mental health and morale and whether they intended to continue with it. This allowed us both to describe the support received and to relate it to various measures of outcome (e.g. whether the foster carer intended to continue fostering and whether he or she did so).

This book is therefore based almost entirely on:

- the initial census of foster carers and a follow-up 17 months later (*n* = 1528)
- the General Questionnaire to the foster carers themselves (*n* = 944).

The content of our questionnaires has been determined by our primary focus. We are not interested in foster care simply as a social phenomenon. Our concern is an applied one. We want to know what can be done to help foster carers. The interventions in which we are particularly interested are those which policy makers can directly control – for example, visits by social workers. They are thus located in the formal system. Our analysis needs to take account of support from 'informal carers' since this is also likely to affect outcomes. Nevertheless our focus is on the support that social services can supply.

As it happens we have covered the topics which Triseliotis and his colleagues found were particularly key for foster carers:

motivation to foster; recruitment; preparation and training; support from social workers and placement or link workers; satisfactions and frustrations; times when they felt like giving up or actually did so and why; the children's parents and contact issues; and views on financial arrangements. (Triseliotis *et al.* 2000, p.9)

All these with the exception of recruitment are covered to a greater or lesser extent in our research. Our conception of support is therefore a broad one. In broad outline we have looked at:

- *Formal characteristics* – frequency of visits from social workers but not measures of the size or density of support networks.

- *Content of support* – adapting a classification introduced by Quinton *et al.* (1998) we have looked at *special interventions* (e.g. training), *emotional support* (e.g. degree to which someone is available when needed and listens), *practical and financial support* (e.g. relief breaks) and *advice/advocacy*. We have also looked at what might be called *negative support* (e.g. the degree to which relatives or neighbours disapprove of the activity of fostering).

- *Sources of support* – we have been particularly interested in formal support from social workers and support for fostering from within the family (e.g. the degree to which the carers' children are behind it). However, we also look at times at support from neighbours, friends, general practitioners, schools and so on.

- *Basis of support* – the basis on which foster carers provide support (in this case more properly described as care) for their foster children: for example, whether they are motivated by altruism or the obligations of kinship and in particular the relative importance of financial and other motives.

- *Outcomes* – we have two broad groups of outcomes. Those concerned with the impact on the child are most conveniently described in the second book. Those concerned with the foster carer include intermediate outcomes – perceptions of support from social services and satisfaction with this – and more 'final outcomes' such as the perceived impact of fostering on family, social and working life, mental health, morale, intentions to continue fostering and whether the carer continued or not.

We have approached the analysis in three steps. First, we have tried to describe the source of support or the nature of the satisfaction or difficulty. Our concern here is with what foster carers say they like and dislike about fostering. Second, we have tried to predict the likelihood that they will be satisfied or dissatisfied, stressed or less stressed on the basis of foster carer or child characteristics. Third, we have examined whether certain interventions tended to produce more successful outcomes than predicted. Broadly, therefore, we have tried to build a 'model' in which outcomes are explained by factors concerned with the foster carer (including the availability of informal support) and by formal support.

A strength of the study lies in the large numbers in some of the samples. This has sometimes made it possible to examine how far our results hold for different subgroups within the sample. Where feasible we have tried to do this. We have also systematically looked for differences between authorities and sometimes within them. In this we hope to contribute to an understanding of foster care that takes due account of its diversity as well as what it has in common.

How the study is written up

This book is written for foster carers, foster children, social workers, administrators, social scientists and all those who take an intelligent interest in foster care. It is also about research and therefore has to justify its conclusions. These requirements are, to some extent, in conflict. It is very difficult to write for a wide audience without cutting out statistical argument and detailed evidence. In facing this dilemma we have tried to write in a way that should be intelligible to anyone while being as clear as possible about the nature of our evidence. We have also tried to be brief.

We have included statistical material. We do not think the latter should deter the interested reader. It is almost always possible to skip the statistics and focus instead on the text. Take, for example, the sentence 'the higher the educational level of the foster carers the less generous they felt the level of payment to be $(p<0.01)$'. The meaning of the sentence remains much the same if the statistical symbol $(p<0.01)$ is removed. Essentially what it adds is the fact that this association was most *unlikely* to have occurred 'by chance'. Assume for the moment that our sample is a fair representation of English foster carers. It is nevertheless possible that in it two characteristics (educational level and a particular view of payment) are associated whereas among English foster carers as a whole they are not. The symbol $(p<0.01)$ says that the probability of this happening by chance is one in a hundred times. Our finding is therefore very likely to be true of the general population. Our advice to the general reader is simply to skip these symbols (and also more complicated ones e.g. Chi square = 3.85, df = 1, $p<0.05$). Occasionally it is necessary to explain some more complicated piece of analysis, as it is central to the argument. Where we believe this to be the case we shall do so.

In relation to content the following three chapters are primarily descriptive. Chapter 2 outlines the social characteristics of carers as part of the task of identifying how they might differ from the general population, and from one another. It considers whether their particular circumstances might affect the way they foster and explores their possible support needs. Chapter 3 gives further information about the carers – the kinds of fostering, such as short-term or respite, that they undertook, information on their fostering 'careers' and the children whom they had fostered. We move in Chapter 4 to the compensations and hassles of fostering – its day-to-day impact on family life, leisure, and finance and use of space.

The next four chapters deal with different reactions to fostering – whether carers see it as having a positive impact, whether they are under mental strain, whether they intend to continue and whether they actually do so. We look at what may influence these outcomes. This includes the carer's social situation, the kind of fostering she (the main carer is almost always female) undertakes, and the events (for example, fostering breakdowns) she experiences. Chapter 7 deals specifically with formal and informal support and Chapter 8 with the differences between those who continue to foster and those who cease doing so. Chapter 9 explores the themes of the chapters immediately before it but uses some rather more complicated analysis. Chapter 10 summarises our findings and discusses our conclusions and recommendations. Some may only wish to read Chapter 10. Others will wish to study the appendices that deal with various technical issues. The book is intended for a wide audience and can be read according to the purpose and interests of the reader.

Chapter Two

Who are the Carers?

Introduction

Support is negotiated in the context of a person's life. One person may need support so that he or she can go out to work. Another may need support in looking after young children at home. By identifying the ways in which foster carers differ from the general population, we can begin to explore the aspects of this context that are important for fostering – the characteristics of, say, a person's family situation, which may make fostering easier or more difficult. This chapter begins this task. Later we shall see that the characteristics that make it less likely that someone becomes a foster carer also make it less likely that foster carers with these characteristics will foster for a long time.

Over the past 50 years there have been three large-scale studies of foster carers in Great Britain. These were carried out by Gray and Parr (1957), Bebbington and Miles (1990) and Triseliotis and his colleagues (2000). In general, this work has suggested that foster families are rather more 'conventional' than others – more likely than comparable families to have two parents of whom one goes out to work, to have somewhat larger houses and to belong to a church. Over the years the proportion of childless couples has decreased – presumably because fostering is less likely to be seen as a kind of quasi-adoption. However, the proportion of foster families with very young children remains less than would be expected from their other characteristics. As discussed in our introduction these studies were prompted by the shortage of foster carers, particularly those for certain groups such as children from minority ethnic backgrounds and teenagers (Caesar *et al.* 1994; Triseliotis *et al.* 2000; Waterhouse 1997). The shortage may be exacerbated by social trends, particularly the increasing involvement of women in the labour market

(Parker 1978) and by the comparatively low supply of foster carers in areas which need them most (Bebbington and Miles 1990). There are issues over the degree to which these problems can and should be overcome through the professionalisation of foster care and more specifically by paying carers a salary, and giving them more training and status. This raises dilemmas. If carers foster for money, are they mercenary? If they do it for 'love', does this mean they are driven by their own needs? In any event it seems that foster care needs more 'non-traditional' carers than have hitherto been recruited.

Against this background this chapter has two aims:

- to compare some of the characteristics of the sample to those found in previous work – particularly that of Triseliotis and his colleagues
- to map out some key dimensions on which foster families vary as a basis for further analysis.

The census: social characteristics of carers

One purpose of the census was to identify differences between those who responded to our questionnaires and those who did not. For these reasons we concentrated on variables which other research or common sense suggested might influence response to questionnaires – for example, educational level and current involvement in fostering. We give below the results for educational level, involvement in work and ethnicity.

Educational level

We asked the family placement social workers to give their view of the educational level of the most educated carer in the foster care household. Farmer and her colleagues (2002) found 45 per cent of her sample of carers for teenagers had no GCSEs. This is of interest as there is some evidence that children whose foster carers have degrees may make better educational progress, at least in subjects other than mathematics (Aldgate *et al.* 1993). As we will see later, educational level is also related to the judgements that foster carers make about the financial support they receive.

In around 200 or 14 per cent of the cases the link family placement workers said that they were unable to judge the educational level. Where they felt able to do so their most common judgement (in 40% of cases) was that no carer in the household had an educational qualification – a figure similar to that obtained in the Farmer study. Professional or degree-level qualifications were noted in less than one in seven cases, a figure that was also similar to Farmer's (12%). There was some evidence that older foster children were more likely to have foster carers with degrees (19% of those whose eldest foster child was 16 or more were said to be qualified at this level as opposed to only 7% of those where the child was under two). Nevertheless, a substantial minority of older foster children did not have foster carers with any qualification. On these figures, foster children intending to take GCSEs will often not have carers able to give them much direct help with their homework.[1]

Table 2.1 Local authority by educational level of foster carer					
	n	Degree (%)	A level (%)	GCSE / O level (%)	None of the above (%)
Area 1	109	25	20	13	42
Area 2	308	17	19	32	32
Area 3	221	12	27	30	31
Area 4	171	9	14	22	55
Area 5	147	9	16	31	44
Area 6	63	22	13	27	38
Area 7	229	7	14	33	46
Total	1248	13	18	29	40

Source: Census 1.
Chi square = 78.3, df =18, $p<0.00001$.

A second striking feature of Table 2.1 lies in the degree of variation between authorities. This could be even more marked within authorities. In Area 2, for example, less than 5 per cent of foster carers in one district but over 31 per cent in another were said to be qualified at degree level. These differences appeared to reflect differences in the social composition of the areas.

Work

As can be seen from Table 2.2, there were equally marked differences in the proportion of foster carers in work. The proportions in full-time work varied from 9 per cent to 27 per cent with an overall proportion of 15 per cent. A quarter was in part-time work with the proportions varying from 13 per cent to 33 per cent. As might be expected, the ages of the children fostered were related to the likelihood that the carer worked. The proportions in full-time work rose steadily from 6 per cent where the eldest foster child was four or under to 17 per cent where he or she was over 16. There was, however, no similar gradient for part-time work. This may be a financial or psychological necessity for some foster carers, irrespective of the age of the child.

	n	Full-time (%)	Part-time (%)	No paid work (%)
Area 1	119	27	13	60
Area 2	338	19	33	48
Area 3	262	14	26	60
Area 4	209	11	19	70
Area 5	147	10	22	68
Area 6	75	17	15	68
Area 7	247	9	25	66
Total	1397	15	24	61

Table 2.2 Local authority by whether main carer has paid work

Source: Census 1.
Chi square = 65.67, df = 12, $p<0.00001$.

These figures are very close to those provided by Triseliotis and his colleagues (2000) for Scotland. They report that 37 per cent of their female carers were in work, which was in 60 per cent of these cases part-time. Our own figures for main carers were that 39 per cent of them were in some form of work, which was in 62 per cent of cases part-time. The relatively high proportion of working carers (in parts of Area 2 the proportion in some form of work rose to over 70%) suggests that support for them may need to include some form of out-of-school or holiday provision.

Roughly one in nine (11%) of our sample were inactive. This meant that they were not fostering and were not expected to do so again. There was a strong association between 'inactivity' and whether the carer was working. Thirty per cent of those who were inactive were in full-time work. The comparable proportion for those currently fostering was only 13 per cent. A high educational level was also associated with 'inactivity'. Eighteen per cent of those with degree-level education but only 9 per cent of those with no educational qualifications were said to be inactive.

The association between high educational level and 'inactivity' was largely explained by the fact that the more highly educated were more likely to have paid work. Among those who worked the more educated were no more likely to be 'inactive' than the less educated. Among those who did not work the more educated were similarly as likely as others to be active. Thus it seemed to be work that led to inactivity. This may reflect a conflict between the two – it is more difficult to foster when working. Alternatively it may have to do with motivation. For example, those who work may be less likely to foster because they need money or because it fits in with their current family circumstances. Either way, the finding suggests a need to take work into account in efforts to increase the pool of foster carers. Recruitment and retention might both be enhanced if either 1. foster care was defined as work (e.g. there was a salary) or 2. it was easier to combine with outside paid work.

Ethnicity

Variations between authorities were particularly marked in relation to the ethnicity of carers. This question was not used in our census in one of the authorities and was not answered in one of the divisions in Area 2. Nevertheless, there was no doubt that major variations existed. Overall 17 per cent of the carers were said not to be 'white British'. Nearly two-thirds of these were said by the link social workers to describe themselves as 'black' and nearly 4 per cent as 'Asian'. Less than 2 per cent were said to describe themselves as 'mixed race' (the term used by us in the questionnaire) although children who could describe themselves in this way are particularly common in the care system.

As can be seen in Table 2.3, the proportion of minority ethnic carers was very low in three areas (varying from 1% in Area 4, to 5% in Area 3). Almost certainly the figures would have been equally low in Area 7. These figures suggest the difficulties that must arise in these areas if a child from an ethnic minority needs to be fostered. However, they are not out of line with what the census suggests as the proportion of ethnic minorities in these authorities. By contrast, the fact that nearly three-quarters of the carers in Area 1 were from minority ethnic backgrounds suggests the potential for recruiting from minority ethnic populations where they exist (see Caesar et al. 1994).

	n	Other ethnic (%)	White British (%)
Area 1	141	72	28
Area 2	328	2	98
Area 3	258	5	95
Area 4	237	1	99
Area 5	154	26	74
Area 6	74	55	45
Total	1192	17	83

Table 2.3 Local authority by ethnicity of carer

Source: Census 1.
Chi square = 512.86, df = 5, $p<0.00001$.

Characteristics of foster families: General Questionnaire

These findings from the census can be complemented by more detailed results from the General Questionnaire. Among other things this covered the composition of the foster carer's family, and certain aspects of their housing and work. We consider these aspects below.

Age and sex of main carer

We asked that the General Questionnaire should be completed by the main carer in the household but suggested that in households with more than one carer they might like to complete it together. In practice the questionnaire was almost always (94% of the time) filled in by women. As will be apparent from the above we have slipped from talking about foster families to talking about the 'main carer' (in practice almost always a woman). This is an almost inevitable temptation in studies of this kind.[2] While this book deals with family issues, it reports them through the eyes of female carers.

The ages of these carers varied from 21 to 75. Most were in their middle years. Ninety per cent of them were between 32 and 57. The average age was 45. The median age was also 45. In other words roughly half the sample were older than 45 and half were younger. This median age of 45 differs little from the median of 47 reported by Gray and Parr (1957) and Bebbington and

Miles (1990). The average of 45 also differs little from the average of 44 reported by Dando and Minty (1987), that of 46 reported by Triseliotis and his colleagues (2000) or of 47 reported by Bebbington and Miles in 1990. In more detail 42 per cent of the carers were in their forties, roughly equal numbers (between a fifth and a quarter) in their thirties and fifties, and very few outside these limits. Triseliotis and his colleagues report very similar figures.

Adults in the family

The majority of these carers (70%) lived in a household with one other adult. A quarter (24%) were lone carers while 6 per cent lived in households with three or four adults. Overall, 74 per cent of the carers said that another adult in the household was their partner, a percentage which is again close to the 70 per cent reported by Bebbington and Miles in 1990 or the 79 per cent reported by Triseliotis and his colleagues (2000) in Scotland. Farmer and her colleagues (2002) similarly report that 69 per cent of their sample were couple carers.

This picture varied with ethnicity. Just over half (55%) of the carers from ethnic backgrounds were lone adults providing care as opposed to 22 per cent of the remainder. The association between ethnicity and adults in the household meant that authorities with high proportions of minority ethnic carers had many more lone carers than others. This may explain why some studies have reported much higher proportions of lone carers than we found (Waterhouse and Brocklesbury 1999). It depends where the research is done. So in this sample calls to diversify the sources of carers have been heeded (at least by some authorities) in relation to ethnicity. There is little evidence of similar diversification in terms of white lone-parent families. As in the case of working carers we shall provide evidence that lone carers have particular needs for support.

Number of children in family

The carers who responded to our questionnaire reported an average of 2.3 children. The figures were very close to those reported by Triseliotis and his colleagues (2000) for Scotland, except that 16 per cent of our sample but only 8 per cent of theirs said they had no children at all. In addition to the carers who had no children, a further 17 per cent appeared to have had a further child after they had begun fostering. Others would no doubt do so in future.

So the decision to foster is obviously not one that is invariably put off until the birth family is in its final form.

Arguably, a more important question concerns the number of dependent children in the household. In this respect, Bebbington and Miles (1990) provide a useful table in which they compare their own sample with the general population sample, standardised to ensure comparable families, and Gray and Parr's sample in 1957. We give in Table 2.4 our own findings, which are quite close to those of both studies. In every row our own percentages lie between the relevant figures given by the two previous studies, a fact which suggests that the differences may have arisen by chance.

A striking example of this consistency is provided by the age of the youngest dependent child. Bebbington and Miles (1990) quote an average age of ten years for this child in their survey – a figure that again differs little from the figure of 9.9 in our own, but is starkly different from the average age of 5 which they quote for the general population. Again this feature of the foster care population seems remarkably consistent in its stability over time and its differences from the general population. We did, however, find more families with no dependent children at home (42%) than did Triseliotis and his colleagues (2000) in Scotland (33%).

Table 2.4 Foster families' dependent children			
	1956[a] (%)	1987[b] (%)	1997[c] (%)
None	49	37	44
One	27	21	23
Two	16	25	19
Three	6	12	10
Four+	2	5	4
All dependent children	100	100	100

Sources: [a] Gray and Parr 1957; [b] Bebbington and Miles 1990; [c] Current study.

Work

The proportion of 'main carers' in full-time work was slightly greater in the general survey than in our census (18% as against 15%) and there were slightly more of them in part-time work (27% as against 23%). These differences may reflect bias or sampling error or the fact that the carers knew more about their working situation than the social workers. In any event the differences are small.

The General Questionnaire survey also provided information on the work of partners. Overall, 70 per cent of these were in full-time work and 8 per cent in part-time work. A further 18 per cent were unemployed. These figures are close to those given by Triseliotis and his colleagues (2000) for male carers, 72 per cent of whom were said to be in full-time work while 22 per cent were unemployed. Our figures for couples suggest that our carers were somewhat more involved in work than those in Triseliotis and his colleagues' sample (2000). In 42 per cent of cases both partners had some involvement in work (often part-time in the case of the woman) whereas the comparable proportion in the Scottish sample was 34 per cent.

Bebbington and Miles (1990) point out that foster families are more likely than the general population to have a traditional pattern of work with only one partner working full-time. They found this pattern in 75 per cent of their foster families where there was an adult couple. This was somewhat less true in our own survey. In 63 per cent of our families, only one partner went out to work, a percentage that excludes the lone carers. In a quarter of the families, no one had full-time employment, and in 12 per cent, both partners were employed. A relatively small proportion (13%) said that they were not working as much as they would wish and that this had to do with being foster carers.

This apparent drop in the percentage of foster carers with 'traditional' patterns is likely to enhance the importance of arrangements for enabling carers to work, or for compensating them if they do not. Work was a key issue for some carers. We look later at its relationship with attitudes to foster care.

Housing

We did not ask the carers about the size of their houses. We did, however, ask if everyone in the household had a bedroom of their own and if so whether this was always so or only sometimes. Overall nearly half (47%) said that this was always so, nearly a third (32%) said that it was sometimes true and a fifth said it was never true. These figures can be compared with those of Triseliotis and his colleagues (2000) who reported that in roughly two-thirds of the cases the most recent foster child had sole use of a bedroom. Both sets of figures suggest that foster children sometimes have to share.

These figures changed quite sharply when we asked what would happen if they did not foster. In that case 83 per cent said that everyone would always have a bedroom to themselves. In a further 7 per cent of cases this would sometimes be true and in only 6 per cent would it never be so.

Unsurprisingly, both sets of figures were strongly related to the number of the foster carer's own children in the house. In situations where there was always a room for everyone the average number of these children was very low (0.6). Where there was sometimes a room for everyone the figure rose (1.2). Where there was never a room the average number was two. As Triseliotis and his colleagues (2000) point out, sharing in all its forms is a sensitive issue for a sizeable minority of foster children. Children who lose sole use of a bedroom because their parents foster may well feel aggrieved.

Attitudes to payment and basic characteristics

Were the basic characteristics of foster carers associated with their views on allowances and fees? This issue clearly bears on the likely effect of increasing fees on the type of carer recruited. We gave the carers four statements and asked them to say how far they agreed with them on a four-point scale (from 'strongly agree' to 'strongly disagree'):

- 'The authority's payment to foster carers is generous.'
- 'The basis on which the authority pays foster carers is fair.'
- 'Foster care is a job of work and should be salaried appropriately.'
- 'Without the fees from fostering we would not continue fostering.'[3]

These statements received very varying degrees of assent (see Table 2.5).

The first two statements attracted the most disagreement. Hardly anyone (5% or less) strongly agreed that they were generously paid or that the basis for payment was fair. About a quarter were prepared to agree that the payment was generous, and around four out of ten that there was a fair basis for it. At the other end of the scale a quarter strongly disagreed that the payment was generous and more than one in six strongly disagreed that it was fair.

The next two statements attracted much more agreement. Forty per cent strongly agreed that foster care was a job of work and should attract a salary. Only one in five disagreed with this statement to some degree and only 1 in 17 disagreed strongly. Just under a quarter strongly agreed that without the 'fees' they would not continue fostering, and a further four out of ten agreed. Only one in eight strongly disagreed with the statement.

	n	Strongly agree (%)	Agree (%)	Disagree (%)	Strongly disagree (%)
Table 2.5 Carers' agreement with statements concerning the finance provided by their social services department					
The authority's payment to foster carers is generous	906	4	26	45	25
The basis on which the authority pays foster carers is fair	903	4	43	34	19
Foster care is a job of work and should be salaried appropriately	911	40	34	20	6
Without the fees from fostering we would not continue fostering	909	24	38	26	12

Source: General Questionnaire.

To our surprise, these statements were less strongly associated with the characteristics of foster carers than we had expected. As we discuss in more detail later the main differences were by local authority. Some authorities were seen as paying more fairly and generously than others. We did not attempt to establish whether or not these perceptions reflected the actual levels of payment by the authorities. The only differences we found by the basic variables discussed above were as follows:

- The higher the educational level of the foster carer, the less generous they perceived the income from fostering to be ($p<0.01$).
- Black and Asian carers were slightly more likely to see the basis of payment as unfair ($p = 0.032$) (possibly they feel that the particular contribution made by their life experience is undervalued).

- Those whose partners were working full-time were somewhat less likely to see the payment as generous,[4] but also less likely to say that they could not continue fostering without the income ($p<0.01$).

- Lone carers were slightly more likely to see the payments as generous ($p = 0.043$).

- Those who were working full-time were slightly less likely to see the payments as generous than those who were working part-time, who in turn perceived them as less generous than those who were not working at all ($p = 0.041$).

These results needed to be treated with some caution. The differences are not large. Moreover, we carried out 24 tests and it would not be surprising if at least one was significant by chance. However, it is unlikely that all the differences arise by chance. Furthermore they suggest a pattern. Those able to command a higher household income (i.e. the better educated, those in work and those with working partners) see the allowance as less generous than others. Conversely, these groups are probably less dependent on the income from fostering as a necessity if they are to foster at all.

Conclusions

The social characteristics of carers varied widely by local authority. Overall, however, there was very little difference between the characteristics of carers in this sample and those studied by Gray and Parr in the 1950s, Bebbington and Miles in the late 1980s, or Triseliotis and his colleagues in Scotland in the late 1990s. The one major difference related to the proportion of minority ethnic carers – a finding that may reflect the fact that we deliberately chose authorities who were likely to have high minority ethnic populations (which Scotland as a whole does not) or a change in practice since the 1980s. The similarity of the four samples is evidence for the national relevance of the present study and for the continuing national relevance of the others.

The similarity between the results of these studies suggests that the characteristics of foster care households reflect more than the 'conservatism' of those selecting carers. The message that there is a need for a wider base for foster care recruitment has by now surely got across. So the fact that carer families are still comparatively unlikely to have young dependent children and a female carer who works full-time suggests that there may be features of the fostering which constrain supply. The mechanism may have to do with motivation – those who want to work may not want to foster – or practicalities – it may be difficult to combine fostering with work, and some fostering schemes require at least one carer to be at home full-time. Whatever the reason, we found that registered carers who were working were much more likely to be seen by the family placement workers as 'inactive'.

One response to these problems would be to make it easier to combine foster care and work (e.g. by providing after-school support). A second, and more widely applicable, response would be to redefine foster care as work, and pay a salary accordingly. This step would not attract universal assent from all carers – a minority, around 25 per cent, would disagree with it. There might therefore need to be recognition that there are different kinds of fostering and that these are undertaken on a different financial basis. A clear and intelligible scheme might help to reduce the sense that the current basis for payments is unfair – something which around half of all carers seem to believe and which is also reported by Triseliotis and his colleagues (2000).

For the moment our findings suggest that financial support is a necessary requirement of fostering. Many carers can only foster because of the financial allowances it attracts. Most, however, do not see the allowances as generous and presumably are not attracted to fostering by its financial rewards. That said, some foster carers do see the allowances as 'more generous' (perhaps the correct phrase would be less niggardly) than do others. The relative financial attractiveness of fostering probably depends on the carers' view of the alternative income they could or do demand. A payment scheme that was designed to treat foster care as work would need to be locally competitive. If it was to be attractive to carers educated to degree level, it might well need to be linked to possibilities for career progression, something that would probably be desirable in any event.

Overall, these findings suggest that support is something that needs to be tailored to the aspirations and situations of the supported. Those who want to go out to work will appreciate after-school arrangements or a type of foster child that enables this to happen. Those who have teenage children may not want an additional teenage child. Those who are lone parents may have particular difficulties if they are ill or need, for some reason, to get away for a short period. Foster carers who are over 50 may not want full-time fostering but might be willing to use their skills in some less demanding role such as that of respite carer. Local authorities differ sharply in the kinds of carer they recruit and therefore in the kinds of support they may need to provide. All need to ensure that this support is tailored to the context of the carers' lives.

Notes

1. Despite this, the figures suggest a rather higher level of educational qualification than those noted for Scotland. There only a minority of carers (17% of men and 20% of women) remained after the official school leaving age, whereas on these figures nearly a third of English carers had A levels or above.

2. For some purposes this may matter less than expected. Triseliotis and his colleagues (2000) found that the majority of their questionnaires (53%) were completed jointly by female and male carers but did not report differences between those completed in this way and those completed by lone (predominantly female) carers. It may be suspected that both sets of questionnaires reflected the perspective of the main carer. Although our authorities differed in their proportions of lone carers this was not the case if the analysis was restricted to white carers. Among white carers the proportions of lone carers was similar across authorities.

3. The use of the word 'fees' as opposed to fees and allowances is, strictly speaking, inaccurate but does not seem to have produced confusion.

4. This was significant on a trend test treating full-time work as 1, part-time as 2, no work as 3 but not significant on the overall Chi square.

Chapter Three

Kinds of Fostering

Introduction

One feature of the 'context of fostering' concerns the characteristics of the carers' families. Another is the type of fostering they provide. This chapter outlines the kinds of fostering undertaken by carers in the sample. It also provides some other related details on the length of time for which they had fostered, the agencies employing them and the basic characteristics of their foster children.

As we will see, the existence of a number of different kinds of foster care is an important element in the logistical problems of providing it. The differences in the kinds of foster care apparently provided by different local authorities emphasise some key issues concerning the kind of foster care that should be provided. Potentially (although in practice less than we expected) different kinds of fostering pose different degrees of stress and require different kinds of support. The pressures under which authorities work may also result in foster carers taking children against their own better judgement – something that we shall suggest is the opposite of supportive.

As in the previous chapter we compare our findings with those of others, particularly those of Triseliotis and his colleagues (2000). The similarities we describe between our sample and theirs again help to emphasise the relevance of their work in Scotland to foster care south of the border.

Some basic data on fostering

Before describing the different kinds of fostering undertaken, we need to give some basic information. Which agencies 'employed' the carers in the sample? How long had they been fostering? How many children were they looking after? We can then see whether the answers to these questions cluster together, so that, for example, more experienced carers tended to be looking after children who had been with them for greater lengths of time.

Agencies and special schemes

Waterhouse (1997) reported that around 2 per cent of 'fostering units' in England were in the independent sector in which she included both voluntary and the 'for profit' agencies. There was, however, a great deal of variation between authorities, with a small number of authorities reporting much higher figures. Our figures were slightly higher than those reported by Waterhouse (2.9% of our sample said they fostered for a voluntary agency and 0.7% for an independent one). The difference may be accidental, a consequence of the authorities in our sample, or of the fact that the independent sector is growing and our study was later than hers. However, in both studies the vast majority of fostering was clearly carried out by foster carers not only registered with the local authority but also supported by it. Since our study there has been further growth in the independent sector (see Sellick 2002).

In one further respect all these local authority foster carers worked within a similar organisational context. All the local authorities supported their carers through specialist teams of social workers responsible for finding placements, supporting the carers and matching carer to placement request. This social work role was distinct from that of the social worker who retained key worker responsibility for the foster child in the placement. This form of organisation now seems to be almost universal in England and Scotland (Triseliotis *et al.* 2000; Waterhouse 1997). The main organisational differences concerned the degree of specialisation. Our authorities could provide this service through one centralised team or through teams divided on a geographical basis.

Carers within the same authority could also experience a different organisational context. They might work for more than one authority – 14 per cent of those fostering for the local authority saw themselves as doing this. The authority might provide different teams for different kinds of work – one authority provided one centralised team to deal with long-term work and another to deal with short-term work. They could also have particular schemes for particular kinds of work – for example, respite care or work with adolescents. Fifteen per cent of the carers said they were in a 'special scheme' and a further 12 per cent that they were not sure whether they were or not. This is a lower proportion than the 33 per cent reported by Triseliotis and his colleagues (2000) for Scotland, but given the uncertainties of definition not too much can be made of this.

Experience of foster care

Experienced foster carers who have taken many foster children or who have fostered for a long time may need less support than newly recruited ones. The number of children previously fostered provides one measure of experience. We asked about this in the general survey. We found that foster carers had fostered on average 19 children apart from those they had when we contacted them (the comparable figure from Triseliotis and his colleagues' 2000 study was 18).

This statistic is somewhat misleading since, as in the Scottish study, the distribution was highly 'skewed'. Around three-quarters of the carers reported fewer than 20, and half reported no more than seven. A quarter of the foster carers were relatively inexperienced, having previously fostered no more than two, and of these nearly a third had taken no foster children before their current ones. At the other end of the distribution, 3 per cent of the sample had taken more than 100 previous foster children and one reported an amazing 543.

The carers' experience in terms of years was also impressive. A quarter had fostered for ten years or more, and of these one had done so for 43 years. At the other end of the distribution, half had fostered for five years or less. Many of these were quite new to fostering. Thirty per cent had fostered for less than three years, a figure which includes 12 per cent who were in their first year. The overall average was 6.9 years. Again these figures are very close to those reported by Triseliotis and his colleagues (2000) who give an average of seven, with 26 per cent having fostered for 11 years or more and 12 per cent for less than one year. In contrast to the Scottish study, however, we did not find that authorities differed significantly in the average length of stay of their foster carers.

If, as national figures would suggest, the number of foster carers has stayed relatively constant over the years, it would be possible to treat those who were fostering in years 4 to 7 as 'survivors' of a larger group who were present in years 0 to 3. Such calculations would suggest that two-thirds of those present in years 0 to 3 should survive to form a cohort in years 4 to 7 and of these two-thirds would again survive into years 8 to 11. A loss of a third over four years (an average of around 9% a year) does not suggest a highly discontented body of carers. This conclusion is supported by the work of

Triseliotis and his colleagues (2000) who give a figure of less than 10 per cent for Scotland and estimate a comparable percentage for England. As we will see, it is also in keeping with data on actual turnover.

Length of time for which children had been fostered

The fact that many foster carers had been fostering for a considerable time does not, of course, mean that they had been fostering the same child. We asked the carers in the general sample to list the foster children in their home (by number not name) and to say how long they had been there. Around a quarter (24%) had been in the home for three months or less and a further 12 per cent for six months or less. Around a third (35%) had been in the place-ment for between six months and two years. The remainder (28%) were equally divided between those who had been in the placement for between two and four years and those who had been there for between four and ten. Only five had been there for longer than this.

This proportion who had arrived within the last six months is greater than might have been suggested by a casual glance at national statistics. In 1994, for example, only around 18 per cent of those looked after had been in the care system for as little as five months or less. This apparent contradiction probably arises because of the difference between time in the care system and time in a particular placement. Around half the moves made by looked-after children may be from one placement to another (Rowe, Hundleby and Garnett 1989).

Age of foster children

Table 3.1 gives the ages of the children fostered as recorded in the General Questionnaire survey. The proportions in different age groups were very similar to those given by Triseliotis and his colleagues (2000) for Scotland and suggested by the comparable figures for England in 1997.

Carers taking children aged less than five differed in some respects from others. They were more likely to disagree strongly with the proposition that caring should be a salaried job (albeit only 10% of them did so – Chi square = 10.36, df = 3, $p<0.01$), much less likely to be at work, and more likely to have other dependent children of their own in the house. They match in some ways the picture of carers who are fond of young children and find that caring for other people's fits their situation while they are at home looking after their own.

Table 3.1 Ages of children fostered		
Age	n	%
0–4	227	22
5–9	297	28
10–15	347	33
16+	177	17
Total	1048	100

Source: General Questionnaire. Not all foster carers returned ages.

Sex of foster children

Overall 46 per cent of the children were female and 54 per cent were male. Where there were two or more foster children in the home there was no obvious policy of either mixing or not mixing the sexes. Slightly more than half these placements involved both males and females – a distribution that would be expected on the basis of chance. Again these figures are very close to those given by Triseliotis and his colleagues (2000) and to figures for the care population in England.

Numbers of children fostered

One in five of the carers in the census were said not to be fostering at the time. Similarly, just over one in six (18%) of those who answered our questionnaire said that they had no current foster child. Triseliotis and his colleagues (2000, p.80) give a figure of 17 per cent of potential carers as not fostering in Scotland at any one time. Overall, there was an average of 1.5 children per registered foster carer and 1.8 for those carers fostering at the time. These figures are somewhat higher than those given by Triseliotis and his colleagues (2000), who give 1.5 for carers fostering at the time, but similar to the figures given by Bebbington and Miles (1990).

Current fostering role

The support needed by foster carers is likely to vary with their role as well as their experience. What kinds of fostering were there? How did these kinds fostering differ in terms of such things as the number and age of children?

What kinds of fostering were there?

The foster carers' roles could be classified in terms of those for which they were approved or those which they actually played. The foster carers' beliefs about their approval status were by no means identical with those of their family placement social workers. Thus an additional classification would be in terms of those for which they believed they had approval. In what follows, however, we have ignored this complexity and taken the accounts of the social workers as the most 'official'.

Official or not, the social workers' descriptions of approvals were difficult to classify. More than 20 different kinds of term were used to describe the nature of the fostering for which the carers were approved. Waterhouse (1997) states that 47 terms were in use among county councils alone. The main variations involved a combination of the length of time likely to be involved (e.g. long-term or short-term), the style or purpose of fostering (e.g. task-centred or relief), the basis of the relationship to the child (e.g. relative) and the characteristics of the child (e.g. teenage or disabled). In addition many carers were classified in more than one way (e.g. as approved for short-term and long-term).

In practice, five main divisions seemed to be involved:

- Long-term fostering – in the main this was described 'long-term', but we included 'specific' fostering where the foster carer was approved for a specific child generally on a long-term basis and fostering preceding adoption.

- Relative fostering – this was as the name implies.

- Short-term fostering – this was usually described as such, but we included within it 'emergency' fostering and the occasional remand fostering.

- Task-centred fostering – the rationale for this fostering was that it would achieve some reasonably specific purpose but we included specialist fostering of teenagers (for example, a scheme for difficult young people based on contracts between those involved and requiring at least one carer to be at home during the day).

- Respite fostering – this was largely, but not exclusively, intended for disabled young people, and we included within it schemes which were community-based but where carers had been registered as foster carers so that they could take young people overnight.

These divisions reflect something of the diverse origins of fostering. This has developed from its original focus on providing long-term care or confronting emergencies (often with young children). The guidance to the Children Act 1989 emphasises the need to consider fostering by relatives. The use of families to provide relief breaks to others has been encouraged by experience in the field of disability. A task-centred approach to fostering has been promoted by the decline in residential care, the professional aspirations of foster carers and the apparent success of some pioneering schemes (Shaw and Hipgrave 1989).

As described above, the distinctions between these categories were not clear-cut. Moreover, carers could be approved for more than one category. Table 3.2 gives the distribution of the groupings we found most convenient. Any carer approved as a relative was classified as a relative fostering. The next four categories in Table 3.2 (long-term, task, relief and short-term) were given if this seemed to be the only classification. The mixed categories were also classified with the priority implied by Table 3.2. For example, if a carer was registered for short- and long-term, she was classified as 'long-term and other' not as 'short-term and other'. One of our authorities approved the majority of its carers for 'task-centred' work. We grouped this with approvals for carers in specialist schemes that seemed decidedly more specialised.

Table 3.2 Registration groups		
Registration group	*n*	%
Relative	109	7
Long-term	342	23
Task	124	8
Relief	120	8
Short-term	357	24
Long and other	145	9
Task and other	108	7
Short and other	112	7
Other	103	7
Total	1520	100

Source: Census 1.

This distribution is very 'approximate'. Major differences between the authorities in the way they classified carers means that if we had adopted different rules for classifying the replies we would have had a very different distribution. The proportion of relative carers is also low compared with that in England as a whole where Waterhouse's study (1997) suggests a figure of around 12 per cent. This may reflect our sample of authorities or the fact that our sampling frame was checked with the family placement teams. Some relative carers may have been supported by social workers in the area teams so that we missed them. As discussed in Appendix 3, a number of carers who described themselves as relatives were not described in this way in our census, being classified, for example, as long-term.

How did the kinds of fostering differ?

Despite its rough and ready nature our classification did relate to some real and important differences. Applying it to the carers in the General Questionnaire survey there were massively significant differences in terms of:

- numbers of children fostered at the time of the survey – from an average of 1.1 with respite carers to 1.9 for those registered for long-term and other (in general, 'mixed' categories had higher averages)

- the average ages of the foster children with the carer – from an average of 7.8 for short-term approvals to 13 for 'task' registrations

- the average length of time they had been there – from 34 months in the case of long-term approvals to 11 for short-term

- the preferences expressed by the carers for short- or long-term work (35% of those approved for 'task-centred work' stated a definite preference against working with short-term cases, as against only 8% of those approved for this work – itself a surprisingly high percentage)

- the average numbers of children previously fostered – from 25.8 for 'long and other' to 0.7 for approved relatives

- the proportion of carers who said they had worked with children with physical difficulties – from 60 per cent for relief carers to 7 per cent for relatives.

A potentially interesting set of differences related to satisfaction with financial arrangements. Relative carers were the most likely to feel financially well-treated, and the least likely to say that they could not foster without the income from it. In many ways relative carers are a particularly interesting group. Appendix 3 summarises some of their particular characteristics and the way they differ from others.

A particularly important set of differences was by authority. Examination of the proportion of carers who were classified as 'long-term' showed that in one authority this was true of 56 per cent of carers, in three authorities the percentage was in the twenties and in three the proportion was 12 per cent or under. These differences almost certainly reflected differences in ideology and nomenclature between the authorities. For example, the authority which approved its carers for task-centred work approved very few for long-term care.

The differences just discussed were rather poor indicators of differences in practice between the authorities. In the General Questionnaire survey there were variations in the average length of stay for foster children in the different households in the different authorities – from an average of 31 months in one authority to 16 in another. However, the authority that had the highest average length of stay approved the second lowest proportion of carers for long-term work.

This difference between the intentions signalled by the categories for approval and the reality of practice probably has various explanations. One of these is the crudeness of our classification. The other, however, is the pressure of reality. As discussed in the second report, some children need long-term foster care. Irrespective of the official position some of them get it. Another part of the reason lies in the pressure on vacancies. We discuss this general form of pressure below.

Pressure

As we have seen, between a fifth and a sixth of the carers had 'vacancies'. In the census, the proportion of carers with vacancies varied between the authorities from 10 per cent to 29 per cent. This figure needs, however, to be treated with caution. Authorities varied in the speed with which they took inactive carers off their list. Some carers with 'vacancies' may therefore not have been available to foster other children. Without an agreed definition of 'active' carer, any comparison of vacancy rates must be very hazardous (see Table 3.3).

What is apparent is that the level of vacancies is almost certainly low relative to need. The problem is probably not so much the absolute level of vacancies but the variety of vacancies that need to be available. All authorities, for example, had some children who had been fostered long-term. The number of carers with vacancies who were approved for this form of fostering either on its own or in combination varied from 0 (two authorities) through 3 or 4 (two authorities) to 14 (three authorities, one of whom may have had more vacancies as one area made no returns). Fourteen vacancies appears at first sight a relatively generous number. It does, however, allow relatively little scope for geography, ethnicity, matching age of foster child to age of other children in the family and so on. For example, one of the authorities with 14 long-term vacancies was subdivided into eight divisions, a number of which had no long-term vacancies at all.

A number of practices seemed likely to be used in attempts to manage the pressures on the fostering system. The most obvious were adoption and determined policies of community care. These were in a sense 'external' to the fostering system and were not covered in this part of the research. Other practices were internal to the fostering system. These included effectively rendering the system unavailable to older children, increasing the average number of children per placement, keeping children for longer than intended in short-term placements, and 'arm twisting' so that foster carers took children whom they did not consider suitable.

Table 3.3 Fostering status of carers by authority				
Authority	n	Currently fostering (%)	Waiting for new placement (%)	Inactive (%)
Area 1	119	76	9	15
Area 2	338	75	13	12
Area 3	262	80	10	10
Area 4	209	90	5	5
Area 5	147	77	9	14
Area 6	75	71	17	12
Area 7	247	83	5	12
Total	1397	80	9	11

Source: Census 1.
Chi square = 38.8, df = 12, $p<0.0001$.

Older children in the system

Our study took place before the recent Leaving Care Act. At that time young
people over the age of 16 might be deemed capable of looking after themselves on their own and as in any case less at risk from their parents. Whether
for this reason or others Area 4 differed from others on its willingness to look
after young people over the age of 16. Only 9 per cent of its foster carers were
looking after young people aged 16 or over as against 33 per cent in Areas 1
and 6 (see Table 3.4).

Table 3.4 Local authority by age of eldest foster child					
		Age of eldest foster child (%)			
Authority	*n*	0–4	5–9	10–15	16+
Area 1	88	13	22	32	33
Area 2	269	10	25	48	17
Area 3	211	13	26	43	18
Area 4	196	25	35	31	9
Area 5	116	14	21	53	12
Area 6	57	12	11	44	33
Area 7	211	8	26	44	22
Total	1148	14	26	42	18

Source: Census 1.
Chi square = 82.3, df = 18, $p < 0.00001$.

Numbers of foster children

The census showed that the authorities also varied in the average number of
children placed with those currently fostering – a figure which ranged from
1.6 to two children per family. Table 3.5 sets out the number of families taking
different numbers of foster children in the General Questionnaire survey.

As can be seen, the most common number of foster children in a family
was one. A quarter of families fostered two children. Nearly a fifth had three
or more and a fifth had none.

Table 3.5 Number of foster children per foster family		
Number in family	*n*	%
0	176	18
1	367	39
2	245	26
3	111	11
4	35	4
5	7	2
All foster children	941	100

Source: General Questionnaire.

In this survey, the foster children were identified only by a number and we had no way of knowing whether they came from the same family of origin. We could, however, tell whether they arrived on the same date – something which would be less likely if they came from different families. Seven out of ten of the foster children in families fostering more than one child did not arrive on the same date.

Placements, preferences and approvals

We compared the length of time for which foster children had stayed in the foster home with the category allocated to them by the family social workers in the census. According to the General Questionnaire survey 234 families had been classified as 'short-term' or mixed 'short-term and other' – a classification which did not include long-term cases. In 50 per cent of these families the foster children had already stayed for an average of seven and a half months or more. The average length of stay was nearly a year.

We also asked the foster carers whether there were certain kinds of children they preferred not to take (see Table 3.6). We gave them a list of 12 possibilities and also asked them whether they had taken such children. Thirty per cent of the foster carers said they had taken at least one. There was some variation between local authorities on this measure with 35 per cent of the carers in the authority that appeared under most pressure reporting such experience as against only 14 per cent in another.

	n	Prefer (%)	Indifferent (%)	Prefer not (%)
Short-term (0–3 months)	711	30	54	16
Medium-term (4–11 months)	671	22	66	13
Long-term	736	40	43	17
Babies/toddlers	692	32	33	35
3–4 year old	674	22	49	29
5–11 year old	724	33	49	18
12 years and over	736	33	27	40
Physical difficulties	630	10	56	34
Learning difficulties	685	16	68	16
Boys	730	23	70	7
Girls	730	30	66	4
Sibling groups	685	19	67	14

Table 3.6 Foster carers' preferences

Source: General Questionnaire.

As others (Farmer *et al.* 2002; Triseliotis *et al.* 2000) have also found, sizeable minorities of carers are prepared to express preferences for or against taking particular types of child. They also expressed preferences over the length of time for which they would keep children. Ideally these preferences are taken into account in matching. In practice pressure can make it difficult to do so. The proportion of carers saying they had taken categories of child they preferred not to take varied from 57 per cent in one authority to 17 per cent in another.

Correspondence between measures of pressure

We considered the following potential measures of the pressure on the foster care system:

- the proportion of vacancies (high means less pressure)
- the mean number of children per placement (high suggests more pressure)
- percentage of older foster children (high suggests less pressure)
- proportion of carers saying they had taken unsuitable cases (high suggests high pressure).

If they are genuine measures, authorities that showed high pressure on one of these measures should tend to show pressure on the others. There was some evidence that this was so (see Table 3.7).

As can be seen from Table 3.7, Area 4 scored consistently high on all these potential measures of pressure, while Area 6 scored consistently low. More generally the authorities with relatively high ranks on pressure on one index had a relatively high rank on the others (Kendal's $W=0.92$, $p<0.001$).

Table 3.7 Measures of 'pressure' in seven authorities				
Authority	Vacancies (%)	Cases per unit fostering	Children 16+ (%)	Mean 'unsuitable' cases per carer
Area 1	24	1.75	25	0.46
Area 2	25	1.68	14	0.44
Area 3	20	1.64	15	0.49
Area 4	10	1.96	8	0.57
Area 5	23	1.86	10	0.49
Area 6	29	1.58	26	0.17
Area 7	17	1.65	19	0.65

Source: Census 1.

Clearly, such measures need to be treated with caution. There are many reasons other than pressure that might lead authorities to score relatively high or low on these measures. That said, they might have value in alerting managers and inspectors to a potentially high degree of pressure where it exists.

Conclusions

The figures we have given in this chapter are very similar to those provided by Triseliotis and his colleagues for Scotland (2000). Our figures for the age and sex of the foster children and the length of service and number of previous foster children taken by the carers are very close. In both countries, foster care is a diverse activity carried out in the main by experienced local authority carers whose commitment is illustrated by their low turnover.

The different categories under which local authorities register their carers illustrate the diversity of the operation but also, perhaps, ideological differences over what fostering should do. The effect of these differences is to some extent overridden by practicalities – the needs of some foster children for long-stay care and the difficulty of making exact matches in a system that has to cater for such diversity.

The overall pressure on the system probably leads to a variety of efforts to manage it. These may include increasing the average number of children per foster family, reducing the proportion of children in the system that are over 16, leaving some children in placements for longer than intended and placing some children with carers who do not feel they are suitable for them.

Chapter Four

Strains and Satisfactions

Introduction

So far we have presented, as it were, the bare bones of the carers' situations. From this we have, perhaps rashly, deduced something about the salient features of fostering for the carers. This chapter takes a more direct approach and relies heavily on the carers' own words. What did they like and dislike about fostering? What kinds of support did they want? The chapter uses a variety of material to tackle these questions, some of it statistical, most of it qualitative and all of it from the questionnaires returned by carers.

In presenting the material we concentrate on the experience of fostering in terms of:

- its impact on family life
- its impact on arrangements (housing, leisure, finance and employment)
- its impact on sense of well-being and satisfaction
- its impact on decision to continue fostering.

As we will see, this material covers much that is important in foster carers' lives. It is obviously likely that carers in different situations will have rather different experiences. Some carers will find fostering easier than others. The issue of how far and why this is so is left to the next chapter.

There are two major areas of fostering which the chapter does not cover. These are 'incidents' (disruptions, accusations of abusing the foster child and the like) and interactions with neighbours, social workers and others outside the family. Both these key areas are covered later in the book.

The impact of fostering on family life

As we have seen most foster carers have children, partners or other adults living with them. Only 14 per cent of the general sample were not living with other adults or with step-children or children of their own. Importing a foster child into such a family can have a major effect on all its members.

We began our enquiry into the impact of fostering on other members of the family by asking the foster carers to respond to the statements set out in Table 4.1. We then asked them: 'Please comment on the effects of fostering on individuals and relationships in your family.'

Table 4.1 Carers' views on effects of fostering on their own family		
Carers' views	*n*	%
Helped our family to get on together	130	14
Not made much difference either way	322	35
Put a strain on family relationships	93	10
Mixed/depends on the child	387	41
Total	932	100

Source: General Questionnaire.

A small number of individuals declined to answer the first question. As one put it: 'I am the family, therefore I alone bear the sole effects of fostering.' Nevertheless, as Table 4.2 shows, the great majority gave replies that suggested that the effect was positive, non-existent or mixed. Those who suggested the effect was mixed felt that it depended on which family member and which of a number of previous foster children were considered. Very few said that the effect was entirely negative.

This picture needs to be qualified in a number of ways. First, those who experience very negative effects on their family are likely to stop fostering. They are therefore less likely to appear in a survey of foster carers. Second, foster carers may not have an accurate picture of how all members of their family feel and may have a vested interest in seeing things positively. Third, bald questions of the type given above have their uses but can capture only a shadow of the feelings that underlie the answers. The qualitative material provided more information about the latter.

Table 4.2 Carers' views on the effects of fostering on individuals in their family		
Carers' views	*n*	%
A basically good effect	371	40
Mixed – depends on individual in family	369	39
Basically a bad effect	15	2
No obvious effect	178	19
Total	933	100

Source: General Questionnaire.

The foster carers' written answers brought out the considerable potential of foster care to affect families for good or ill. Some respondents saw the impact as entirely positive:

> We all enjoy fostering and it is a job which suits me and my family.

> We just love the job we do and we have fostered all our married life.

Others saw things at least for the moment in a more negative light:

> Fostering has put a strain on our whole family relationship. I am much more easily stressed and the children are much more difficult individually as well.

> I feel that people do not fully appreciate the family tensions of a difficult placement.

Others were more philosophical, observing that much depended on the child placed with them and that even if some members of the family were stressed others would take up the strain:

> Relationships and effects of fostering within the family vary with the child placed. In very difficult placements it can be a very stressful and unrewarding time for all family members. But other times can be very different.

Sometimes my husband and I argue when we are struggling with a difficult placement. My children, however, are the best children I know, they are kind, thoughtful and mature.

A number of factors seemed to influence the nature of these impacts.

Support from family for carer

The effect of a supportive family was undoubtedly important:

We have a large loving and close family and whether we had ten foster children things would be no different, as being a mother and a father is a doddle.

Family members could support the foster carer's belief that what they were doing was worthwhile, and provide practical and emotional support:

Both our daughters who were fostered before being adopted are very supportive with our placements. One long-term foster child enjoys children coming into our home with the knowledge that he is staying permanently.

My husband is the most important source of support I get because we discuss everything about the foster children and work very closely together.

In these respects the extended family and former children who now live away could all be important. The latter in particular could support their parent(s) in their desire to foster or feel that it represented too much of a strain or a diversion from their role as grandparents:

Daughters think it is too much now and we should be packing it in. Extra work involved, worry about child etc.

My family are all married now and are supportive but one son feels we should give more time to our grandchildren.

My own children visit less since my last placement, especially the one with my grandchild.

Children in the home could be a help in the fostering process itself – helping with the foster children, making them feel at home and inducting them into the ways of the household:

My family, my sons and daughter involved my foster children from the start, they took them out and involved them and never made out they were any different from anybody else.

My children have been very supportive and caring. They take part in settling children who come into care. Especially white kids as we are Asian/Sikh foster carers.

We all work very hard as a family to help them feel loved and cared for and soon they feel worth something.

Fit between fostering and family life

A key issue for the family was the degree to which fostering fitted in with its current situation. For some fostering fitted in well:

I enjoy the challenge of being part of the care process. Also it allows me to bring in income which allows me to be here for my own children.

We usually only foster respite placements and these placements are often few and far between, so we are not under any strain or stress for long. I also child-mind so fostering fits in very nicely with our lifestyle.

With others, however, the fit was more problematic. Most of the reasons are discussed in more detail later, when we deal, for example, with the impact of fostering on outside work. However, the perceived need to work arises in part from the 'life stage' of the family and had its place in family priorities:

My husband is working long hours – starts very early, 5–6 in the morning and arriving home at 6–7 o'clock. We have to look carefully at the child's needs and how they fit in with the household. It restricts how much input we can supply towards the young person's social life and development.

Financial worries. Changes in family circumstances. Older child starting secondary school out of area. Travelling worries. Older daughter just started college has to be supported financially.

A second priority was the needs of natural children and partners:

At the moment the age gap between the fostering children and our own children is large enough not to affect them but as they get older we can see this being a problem.

We now have a young child of our own and would have to see what effect fostering has on her. She did not get on with the last little girl but perhaps that was because there was only six weeks difference in ages.

As my family grows time spent together becomes more important and yet fostering places a large demand on the time available.

The lack of time was an example of difficulties between family members over sharing. The objects to be shared – rooms, attention, time, clothes and other property – varied. The common element was that there was not enough to go round. This could involve foster children:

Before fostering I was unaware of the jealousy – perhaps that is too emotive a word – which could be engendered because of the time needed to be spent with children particularly when they first arrive, aware that they are only with me for a short time.

It could also involve family members:

All have experienced some problems in sharing me including my husband.

Our children have learnt to share us and everything else with the foster child in our care.

Daughter would like home to herself sometimes as shares room. As now 16 would like more time.

One carer faced with these problems felt that she had to be forceful to get some time for her own children:

In the three and a half years I have been fostering I have never put any of my fostered children into respite. This year I am doing so ... I feel I have had to be strong to stand up to this and have got through by saying that my own children need quality time with their mum.

A further issue concerned the need for 'normality'. Many saw fostering as being as pre-eminently normal as having a 'big' family:

Usually the foster children fit in and are accepted by our children – occasionally difficulties but no more than one would expect in a large family – we have no complaints of one child getting special treatment.

> She fits in like a piece of a jigsaw, it's a pleasure.

A minority, however, seemed constrained:

> Our major concern is fostering a child that has suffered some abuse and been involved in inappropriate sexual behaviour herself. We don't know how to protect ourselves from accusation without leading a totally different and restricted lifestyle. It is difficult to be 'normal'.

The age and state of health of the carers were also important:

> We will probably give up fostering over the next two years as our charge is expected to go into residential schooling. Also we are both over 60 and less likely to take on another child.

Problems from the difficult behaviour of foster children

These difficulties, connected with feeling that there was not enough to go round, could be exacerbated by the attachment difficulties and behaviour of foster children:

> Another child would not respond to my daughter's overtures but everywhere I went she was right behind me. It was quite trying.

> My own children didn't like the whole attention one child demanded.

Feelings of jealousy were not confined to foster children and some foster carers acknowledged there might be a realistic basis for children feeling 'left out':

> One [of our children] expressed jealousy which went undetected for approximately 15 years.

> My last natural child at home has been treated differently from the others because of my lack of time for him and a certain amount of disruption in his life.

> Girls got on all right. Son resented it a little as foster child damaged his property.

Difficult behaviour could create problems for all:

> My son who is 16 finds it hard to cope with lads who I foster when they steal his things or clothes. Apart from that my son and daughter usually get on with all ages of kids we foster.

> My long-term foster daughter had her necklace stolen by another child when she left. I am still trying to get it back…they just keep on passing the buck. In my opinion they are only telling my foster daughter 'take what you like, wait long enough and you get away with it'.

In addition to theft, other difficult behaviour – for example, bullying, destructiveness, 'stirring', verbal abuse and false accusations – could all cause problems:

> Poor behaviour and mood swings have a bad effect on the family. My daughter finds it very difficult when objects in the house get broken.

> Own children have been subject to violence and effects of foster children's anger and needs – feeling of always having to share – no family time without other children.

Difficulties could also arise because foster children were seen as leading the carers' own children astray:

> Sometimes I find my daughter copies behaviour which I don't like from my foster children.

> Made no difference to me. Daughter picked up all foster child's bad habits.

Problems of loss

An unexpected, but in a way obvious, difficulty could arise from the need for the family to care without attachment. Whereas this goes, in a sense, with the job for adult foster carers, there has been little attention to its possible implications for the carers' own children:

> Our sons are very caring towards foster children. They get very upset when a young child stays for 19 months and becomes part of the family but has to move on to long-term care.

Overall impact on children

Overall, and very much on balance, most of the foster carers who talked about the long-term impact of fostering on their children felt that it had been good. The benefits were in learning about the misfortunes of others (hence perhaps also becoming more appreciative of their own parents) and becoming more caring and better able to share:

> It has taught my children that there are people out there who haven't had all the benefits they have had i.e. happy, loving, caring homes. It has taught them to appreciate the good things in life.

> I sometimes wonder if my natural born children would be different if they hadn't seen and experienced some of the negative stuff, especially my little girl, but on the whole I think it's given them a sense of caring for others and a greater understanding. Unfortunately one of them is considering becoming a social worker!

> As a family it's not just my own family but my grandchildren who keep us in touch with the young people that pass through our life, all the young people we have cared for over the years. The grandchildren have gained a caring and better understanding of the less fortunate children and in some cases real friendships have developed.

In some cases foster children were seen as providing an object lesson in the consequences of poor behaviour:

> Fostering has hugely helped our children. They themselves have very firm boundaries and have passed this on to foster children. We believe children learn better from children. Thus they don't want adults to keep on at them.

> The effects of fostering in my family are good in the main unless the foster child is particularly demanding. Fostering has had a good effect on my own two children, they have learnt a lot from foster children about what not to do, and the effect it has on them when they have misbehaved.

So good habits, as well as bad ones, may apparently be learnt, if not necessarily in the same way. The foster children themselves may not have been so enthusiastic about being object lessons in morality but we do not know what they thought.

Overall our research, based though it is on parent reports, supports the findings of smaller studies which have involved interviews with children

(Ames Reed 1993; Kaplan 1998; Pugh 1996) as well Triseliotis and his colleagues' larger study based on parent reports (2000). Like these other researchers we have found that for birth children fostering is a mixed experience, one which raises issues of sharing and which may require children to exercise tolerance beyond their years but which on balance seems to contain more positives than negatives. As Farmer and her colleagues (2002) also found, birth children can also be a major source of support to parents who foster.

Impact of fostering on living arrangements

Fostering affects other aspects of the main carer's and the family's life. Its potential impacts cover housing, leisure, family finances and employment. We asked the foster carers to rate the impact of fostering on these aspects of family life and then to comment briefly on why they made the ratings they did.

As can be seen from Table 4.3, carers most commonly suggested that fostering had either had no effect or that it had a mixed or neutral effect – altering, for example, the way that a house was used rather than rendering it more or less good from the point of view of the residents.

Table 4.3 Carers' views on the practical effect of fostering on areas of family life					
Carers' views	n	Good (%)	Mixed/ neutral (%)	Bad (%)	No obvious effect (%)
Housing	912	13	34	7	46
Leisure	906	15	41	24	20
Finance	905	14	47	12	27
Employment	883	6	29	11	24

Source: General Questionnaire.

Housing

One carer felt that there were few problems in any of the areas we had identified. This was because of her overall situation:

We have a large house with lots of space. This is a must for children – lots of sporting activities i.e. swimming every week, rugby, cricket, cycling etc. Finances are not too bad as we have no mortgage. Being self-employed work has much improved.

Another felt that she could not answer in general:

I feel that the individual child affects the four areas above.

Others felt that these issues were in the overall scheme of things of relatively little importance:

I enjoy having the children around.

Those who saw problems in the area of housing concentrated on three main areas – wear and tear, lack of space, and niggardly or tardy financial assistance either to repair damage or improve the house from the point of view of the foster children.

The effects on the house were strongly felt by some:

Home has been destroyed, doors kicked in, wear and tear enormous with almost no compensation.

They destroyed property. No compensation for decor, wear and tear of property.

Space was mentioned less often than might have been expected, given the number of children who could not have a bedroom to themselves:

Problems of space frequently encountered as we often take sibling groups but would still prefer to keep them together.

Some carers had taken steps to rectify this situation:

The finance we receive is usually put back into the house to make more space or make life easier for the foster children with special needs.

Foster carers who had done this without financial help from the local authority were sometimes resentful:

I bought my own seven bedroomed house to be able to provide more comfort for all my children (at great expense) – my local authority grudgingly gave me £200 towards removal expenses.

Housing – paid £20,000 ourselves to facilitate loft conversion – no assistance from local authority.

Leisure

Carers commenting on the impact of fostering on leisure generally stressed the negative effects. This could give a misleading impression. As seen earlier, only a quarter of the sample actually rated the overall impact as negative. Negative effects are, however, more noticeable and easier to describe.

Whatever else it does, fostering reduces the amount of time available for other things. One carer who had fostered two children over six weeks in the school holidays had:

Found it difficult to fit in normal things like shopping, cleaning, going to the bank. Couldn't afford to go to theme parks, zoos, entertainment places because no money to pay for foster children.

Despite the above some carers commented that there had been no effect on leisure:

Leisure time shared by my family has not been affected. The foster child in our care is included in everything we do.

Another agreed that there was an effect on leisure but discounted it:

With being a single mum with two children and three foster children I certainly don't get a lot of leisure time. But I wouldn't do the job if I didn't enjoy it or feel it was worthwhile.

Others felt that leisure was inevitably, and perhaps rightly, sacrificed:

A working mum is stretched many ways between our children and partner and extended family. Foster children need more quality time and therefore carers sacrifice any free time they may otherwise have had.

Fostering is a full-time, 24 hour a day job…leisure time is something you take when you can.

Others, however, felt that they sacrificed too much leisure and that the local authority should do something to rectify the situation:

Fostering affects strongly my social life. There should be a free service available which provides care for the children for a day/weekend.

The placement I have at the moment can be very difficult. Our hobby was going away on fishing trips at weekends before. We have tried to continue but have found it totally impossible and we have not been offered the respite care we were promised.

Some wanted overnight and others less extended breaks. The reasons given included the incessant demands of fostering, and the need to recoup:

Leisure time basically none as 24 hours care and supervision is required. Carer's life is on hold and freedom of carer's space is non-existent.

The occasional weekend away would be nice to recharge our batteries.

Some commented on the particular difficulties of arranging such breaks through the usual means employed by parents:

Appropriate adult care if we want an evening out together.

Baby sitters are hard to find for some of the children we foster; I usually have to rely on my own family because the kids we foster are hard to handle, sometimes.

Some carers commented on the particular circumstances in which breaks were wanted:

When difficult children in placement affected my employment, also leisure time.

We have an autistic child so sometimes going out is difficult.

Leisure times are difficult and often spoilt by a difficult and moody child.

Others commented on the impact of financial considerations:

We do not have enough money or adequate transport to have much leisure time as a family.

Leisure time can be difficult due to baby sitting. Out of pocket allowances does not cover the cost of taking out foster children e.g. cinemas, outings, cubs or scouts events.

A rather small number of carers felt that fostering had enhanced their leisure time:

> Fostering has helped us to enjoy living with children around with more money for leisure time as a family.

> Given us a more active lifestyle.

> I am a single person so the effect on me has been good and I have enjoyed fostering.

The last carer quoted emphasised the enjoyment of fostering. This was a point that many others made in a different section of the questionnaire. As we will see, many find fostering very enjoyable most of the time:

> I just love taking care of the children and find them real fun to be with – just doing things together.

Most, however, did not define such enjoyment as 'leisure time'.

Finance

As we have seen, there were disagreements among carers about the importance of payment but the majority did feel that fostering was a job of work that should be properly rewarded. Nevertheless, some felt that the compensations outweighed the financial loss:

> Fostering children fits in with my lifestyle and gives me nothing but pleasure. I enjoy it and do not think of fostering as a job of working toil.

> I am happy with the payment. I have no strong feelings at present as I am devoted to my foster child.

Such carers were critical of those who saw a problem over financial allowances and resented those who imputed mercenary motives to foster carers:

> Couples who foster should remember this job is voluntary.

> Some members of my family have said we went into fostering for the money. The money is irrelevant.

Others felt that the financial payments were too low. Some supporters of this view appealed to pragmatic arguments. They saw the money as insufficient either to enable a decent service to the children or to attract new carers:

> In order to look after the children to a high standard which they deserve the payments need an overall review as I feel they are too low and do not give encouragement to new carers.

A more common argument appealed to standards of decency and fairness:

> As a foster carer we would like to see some benefits for foster parents as this is a lot of hard work on a family especially when you have difficult children.

Some of those making this point emphasised the difference between looking after a family and carrying out the bureaucratic tasks and unusual risks entailed by foster care:

> I do think fostering should be classed as a proper job with wages paid to a foster carer as it is hard, demanding, time consuming, not just taking care of the children but they also have to deal with contact for the family, meeting with social workers and a lot more people in their own homes. Any allowance is for the placement and most is cancelled out by the needs of the placement. Very little is left over for treats etc.

> I sometimes think – is the possibility of a false allegation of abuse by a child in our care worth all the hassle – pay very poor.

Some emphasised the impact on other employment – a point dealt with more fully in the next section:

> Family finance depleted, employment minimal.

Others made points about the 'conditions of service' – the lack of holiday pay (a point one carer felt particularly affected black families), pay when children are not present and the absence of pension provision or qualifications which can be used in other jobs later (a point dealt with in the next section):

> Different boroughs make different rules not all of which are fair i.e. we are made responsible for these children and totally entrusted to look after, protect and counsel them. We are not financially rewarded for the after-care or given pension or holiday money for ourselves or respite.

> Lack of funds from the local authority prevents me from taking my usual annual holidays abroad. This affects most placements with black families who regularly visit their families abroad.

> We should be paid a fee when we don't have a placement. As we can't work we are just waiting around. We lose out. Also we are not allowed to work for other boroughs or agencies. Sometimes we have gone six months without a placement.

Others made points about the particular costs and difficulties associated with some children and the lack of adequate recompense for taking them:

> Extra washing and use of tumble dryer to keep wet beds clean and dry.

> Finance is poor. Our foster children were banded for their difficult behaviour but social workers changed banding allowances without consultation and although we have applied for project fostering for their behaviour we have been told it is not for children with difficult behaviour.

> I think you should be paid higher for the new born up to the age of one year as they are a lot more expensive at this age with all the things they need and the way they grow out of their clothes every few weeks.

Employment

The perceived impact of fostering on work clearly depended on whether or not the foster carer wanted or needed to go out to work, and if so on the kind of outside work she did. It also depended on the relative importance that the carer gave to outside work:

> Fostering is only part of our life. I have a demanding and stressful job which dominates a lot of my/our time. Fostering has to try and fit round us.

Some pointed out that their need to work affected the kind of child they could take:

> As a single carer I have to consider whether the child to be placed will be affected by my need to work. Although I am trained as a teacher and this fits in with children in mainstream education, it is not always possible to take on children who are excluded from school for financial reasons.

The fit between schooling for the children and outside work for the foster carer was causing problems for another carer:

> Full-time employment and shifts is causing problems with inset days, after school care/money involved.

Some carers cut down their work in response:

> Cut my work down by days a week – still asked to work less time during school holidays.

> At first I had to give my job up as my placement can't be left on his own with my husband. I now work for a couple of hours in the afternoon.

The need for transport for the foster children and for the foster carer caused problems for others. The demands for transport can be heavy, particularly perhaps in more rural areas:

> Recently we have fostered three young children and at the moment I have to taxi them to school nursery each day which has meant I am driving about three times a day – 10 miles return each time.

Not surprisingly, this can cause problems that may be compounded by the need to attend meetings connected with foster care on weekdays:

> My husband finds that meetings with social workers during the day Mon–Fri place a pressure on him as he has to re-schedule his work day.

> Both our employment has suffered due to the necessity to attend meetings and have our own children (below school age) cared for at these times. Also arranging transport has been difficult as we have one car only.

Others made comments similar to those of the teacher at the beginning of this section emphasising their need to work and the potentially negative impact of certain kinds of fostering on their ability to do so.

One emphasised the lack of qualifications:

> As a long-term foster carer apart from the excellent training with National Children's Homes I have no work record, normally 20 years work record would give some security.

Others said they were thinking of leaving foster care:

> Because of financial commitments and the need for more secure employment.

Or because:

> I want to find a job with more hours in order to support us. Also so I can socialise with adults for a change.

These decisions were not necessarily motivated by dissatisfaction with foster care. One commented that:

> If I go back to full-time work it would restrict my role as a foster carer so I may change to a respite carer.

Another faced:

> Possibility of being made redundant – then I'll have to find another job which may not fit in with fostering.

Impact of foster care on sense of well-being

Given that fostering has a number of disadvantages for foster carers, why do they do it? The reason seems to be that most of them gain great satisfaction from it. Evidence for this came from three questions that we put to foster carers about their overall attitudes to fostering and the satisfaction they got from it. Table 4.4 sets out the replies.

Table 4.4 Carers' views on the response of their family to different aspects of fostering					
Carers' views	n	Strongly agree (%)	Agree (%)	Disagree (%)	Strongly disagree (%)
We get a lot of satisfaction from fostering	924	46	51	3	0
Fostering enriches our lives	903	31	57	11	1
Everyone in this family is pleased we foster	902	27	55	16	2

Source: General Questionnaire.

As can be seen nearly half the sample strongly agreed with the statement that they got a lot of satisfaction out of fostering. A mere 3 per cent disagreed with it. The other statements elicited slightly less emphatic endorsement.

Nevertheless, it seems obvious that most of the main carers feel that they get a lot from caring. Foster carers explained their lack of strain and overall level of satisfaction in varying ways. Some attributed it to their temperament and personality:

> Always been this way.

> I am usually a happy person and try to make the best of whatever arises.

> I am as happy and in control as I have always been.

Others explained that they were used to fostering or that they had realistic expectations of it and so avoided disappointment:

> We have done it so long it is part of our life.

> I don't get very worried about things. As a whole I am a pretty easy going person because I feel I can only do as much as these children can let me do.

Much more commonly, however, they simply said they enjoyed fostering. The words 'enjoy' or 'enjoyment' continually recurred. The reasons for this enjoyment were variously put. Some said they loved being a mother or loved children:

> I enjoy fostering and I enjoy playing the role of their mother.

> I just don't know what to do if I don't have children to mind. I love them being here and we do a lot of good for them.

Others took up the point made at the end of the last quotation and emphasised the satisfaction that was gained from helping people, using skills and responding to need:

> I have always worked with children and feel I can contribute something to the lives of those who stay with me.

> I feel I am doing something worthwhile for someone who needs me and if I can help that child feel wanted and loved and be part of our family it is well worth the affection and love they give back and that is satisfaction enough for me.

Such carers acknowledged that fostering met a need to feel that they contributed and led useful lives:

> I feel it meets needs within myself. I enjoy the challenge [a word that, like 'enjoy', recurred].

> Because fostering makes me feel good about myself. Because I enjoy what I do.

> It's my need. 'I want to help others.' Anyway I like children and find fostering very rewarding…it makes me happy and sometimes very sad but that's how it goes.

Some seemed to get their fulfilment from their work with particular children – in a small number of cases because these were relatives:

> I recently started to have quality time with my new respite foster child. I look forward to our outings together. He is a very special young man and I am so pleased we have met.

> It gives me great satisfaction to see the child I have at the moment feel loved and wanted. Her smiles and laughs says it all.

> The only reason, possibly, my partner and I are fostering is because the children we care for are our grandchildren. Therefore their well-being, health and happiness comes before our needs.

These particular satisfactions could engender great commitment:

> We have two lovely little girls who need us and we are willing to look after them until they don't need us anymore.

> Because my boys are long-term I will continue to foster them in adulthood and forever if they need us.

These satisfactions enabled many carers to ride the stress:

> Just makes life worthwhile, doing something that makes me happy. Sometimes it's hard but I have a laugh, a cry or a scream and carry on.

Others felt that there was little stress to ride:

> As a link carer I only do one weekend a month and although I feel good about what I do it doesn't affect me too much.

At present I am on the sidelines of fostering. If I had been answering this questionnaire last year my answers would have been totally opposite probably. As it is I have regular visits…from those I have fostered. I think single parents are an asset to particular problem children but they do need a great deal of support which I am still lucky enough to receive.

Others, however, experienced and reported great strain:

Fostering is a 24 hour job, it is accepting 95% to 100% responsibility for the young person in your care. Dealing with doctors, dentist, school, their parents and family also their friends. It is about giving a great deal and perhaps not getting anything in return, not even a thank you. It can be attending every police station and courts around the area one time. It's about opening your home to all different strangers. It's about being short of cash all the time. Carers can and do get burnt out.

The reasons for this experience of strain were, to some extent, the mirror images of those used to explain satisfaction. Some carers saw themselves as not blessed with an easygoing temperament:

Because as a carer I'm forever worrying I am doing the best for my children.

The baby has not been well. He is teething and appears to have ongoing fevers and ailments, has regular check-ups, doctors say 'no need to worry'.

Others were in inherently stressful situations. One carer, for example, did not have the large house, garden and other resources that were deemed essential by one quoted earlier. She commented that:

With three young children in a first floor flat it's a bit of a strain at the moment and is very exhausting at times.

More commonly, carers complained of the strain produced by particularly difficult foster children who did not fit into the family like pieces in a jigsaw:

It gets very difficult at times when you have a 15-year-old boy with a mental age of 9 who fluctuates between 9–15 and who has a reading age of 6 and is bone idle. Because of adolescence won't get bathed and has to be made to get a shower at school.

> We are having difficulties with all foster children. Twins' natural mother (they don't have contact) has had [major surgery]. Our son has been *accused* of sexual abuse against another boy.

> We have experienced bad dreams, wet beds, breaking things, exposing himself to neighbours. It's been quite hard for all of us.

> Because one of the girls we foster is causing so many problems and the police are involved and social services. We don't feel we have time or space for anything else.

Such children brought their carers unhappiness rather than delight. Rather than two lovely little girls one carer had experienced:

> One boy of…years who has been sexually abusing his own sister and has had rather an impact on my feelings. I feel very sorry for him and his lovely family. It was very sad and upsetting to see all the suffering it was causing everyone.

> Looking after a depressed child is very depressing. And constantly being called names and being on the receiving end of violence is demoralising.

In such situations the carers did not necessarily feel the sense of usefulness that other carers experienced – quite the reverse:

> Because sometimes I can't see the difference in the foster child.

This feeling of inefficacy could be reinforced if the carer felt devalued by others:

> At present I'm feeling a lot of unhappiness with fostering. I often feel useless and as though my hard work is not seen or my opinions are not listened to. Maybe resources are to blame…I'm powerless.

Moreover, the commitment of carers to their foster children that brought joy to some could bring grief to others when the children left:

> Because I had three brothers for five months and they had to go to another foster home to be assisted and I really miss them. That's why I get upset and feel unhappy sometimes.

> Because in February we lost a child to adoption very dear to our hearts or my own at least and have been grieving for this child, therefore leaving

me depressed on occasions and feeling whether it was all worthwhile…
me and my family are strained by the ups and downs of fostering due to
recent events. I don't feel I get the buzz I used to get or satisfaction from
it. I feel very strongly that carers are sometimes made or expected to be
like robots – my main concern is for people like myself who have suffered
a loss as nobody asked me if I need counselling or would like some counselling – maybe they can't offer this, I don't know.

And irrespective of the stresses of fostering it has to be remembered that foster
carers are no more immune than others to the bereavements, illnesses, redun-
dancies and family disruptions that constitute the psychological hazards of
ordinary life:

> Recent problems relate to issues in our own family.

> The reason for our feelings to date has to do with an accident to our
> daughter which has created problems for *all* the family.

Sometimes these strains are cumulative, the stresses of fostering adding to
those that would in any case have had to be faced:

> In the last 10 months I have lost four relatives through death. My worst
> loss was that of my father. My mother has been unwell and was recently
> burgled so I am extremely anxious for her welfare. I also had a foster child
> that had been with me for two and a half years move on.

Impact on decision to continue fostering

One justification for supporting foster carers is that it may reduce turnover.
For this reason we asked foster carers if they had ever thought of giving up
fostering and also whether they intended to do so over the next two years.
Answers to the two questions were naturally associated and are set out in Table
4.5. As can be seen, only 7 per cent of the carers said that they would definitely give up over the next two years, although nearly a third said that they
might do so.

Most of those who were thinking of leaving had previously thought of
doing so at least sometimes. However, a minority said that they only rarely or
even never entertained this thought but might nevertheless leave in the next
two years. Broadly the qualitative replies could be divided into six main
groups:

Group 1   Considered stopping because of age or poor health although some of these might undertake forms of fostering which they saw as less demanding (e.g. respite).

Group 2   Intended to stop when a foster child to whom they were particularly committed left.

Group 3   Considered stopping because of a change of circumstances (e.g. the need to get a better paid job or children growing up).

Group 4   Were dissatisfied with fostering or stressed by it or foresaw that a particular foster child would become too much for them in the future

Group 5   Intended to continue fostering but only because of a particular child or children.

Group 6   Were committed to fostering and would continue to do so.

Table 4.5 Previous and current thoughts on leaving foster care				
		Over the next two years will you give up foster care?		
Have you ever felt you would like to give up foster care?	*n*	Yes (%)	Not sure (%)	No (%)
Very often	31	45	42	13
Often	81	17	52	31
Sometimes	356	6	47	47
Hardly ever	217	4	18	78
Never	253	3	13	84
Total	938	7	32	61

Source: General Questionnaire.
Chi square = 237.7, df = 8, $p<0.00001$.

In general, the reasons for commitment and dissatisfaction are those we have rehearsed above. In one respect, however, the questions about leaving introduced a new cause for dissatisfaction – namely a feeling that social services did not listen to and respect foster carers or treat them as part of the caring team. Three carers can represent a number:

> Foster carers are not told the whole truth about placements very often. We are also not treated as part of the team by social workers. Too many student workers who are left to do the job but have not got enough experience.

> The problem I am having is with the social worker who does not have any respect for my family and will not communicate properly with us.

> Sometimes I feel you are at the bottom of the pile. Everyone's views – child/parents/social worker – seem to come first.

Conclusions

This chapter has produced few numbers and much comment. For these reasons it cannot provide a quantified account of the problems of foster carers and the scale of the effort that would be needed to support them properly. It does, however, make use of the insights of foster carers themselves and can, we believe, provide hypotheses on the kind of support carers need. This support would need to cover a number of areas.

First, most, but not all, foster carers see fostering as a job that should be appropriately rewarded. This view of foster care has implications for fees and allowances. The more adequately these foster carers are rewarded, the higher their morale is likely to be. For other foster carers, reward is less important but there is no evidence that their morale would be eroded by higher fees or allowances. Other considerations that arise from this view of foster care include the possibility of pensions and the desirability of qualifications that would equip the foster carer for other work if he or she wanted to do it.

Second, foster care takes place in a family context. The children placed with the foster carer need to be of a kind that suit this context and the predilections of the foster carers themselves. This means, for example, that there may be difficulties in placing children who are close in age to the foster carers' own and who may compete with them. Similarly some foster carers feel they are too old to cope with teenagers, some welcome a challenge, some want children who will go to school so that they can go to work and so on. It does seem that foster carers, particularly experienced ones, can think through issues of this sort in advance. It should be possible to respect their wishes.

Third, foster care influences and is influenced by a variety of social arrangements and circumstances – not least the housing, leisure, employment and financial position of the main carer. In these respects, the expectations as well as the circumstances of carers seem to differ widely. A truly supportive system would take these expectations and circumstances into account. It would recompense carers whose house had been damaged by their foster children and do so quickly and without undue quibble. It would respond quickly when, for example, travel arrangements or children's illness were making it difficult for a carer to go to work. It would involve negotiations with the carer over alterations to housing, and ensuring that holiday times did not conflict with the carer's work when this was important to her.

Fourth, fostering can be invasive and stressful. A supportive system would tackle the sense of foster carers that they have been left holding the baby – for example, by ensuring effective 24-hour cover. It would enable carers who felt they needed it to have occasional breaks to recharge their batteries. It would deal with the sense of uselessness that some carers report by sensible reassurance and respect. It would recognise the extremely difficult behaviour with which carers are confronted and provide them with ways of understanding it and attempting to handle it. It would respond, perhaps through counselling, to the grief and disturbed feelings that can arise in carers when they lose or feel they have failed children to whom they are committed. It would not place very difficult children with carers where there did not seem to be reasonable possibility of success.

Fifth, the reasons that some carers gave for continuing to foster seem linked to having a particular child still placed with them. To improve retention, a supportive system may need to pay particular attention to the needs of these carers when these placements come to an end.

Support, in short, should not be seen as a standard set of routine measures. Rather it is likely to be an imaginative, practical and prompt response to an accurate perception of a carer's situation as the carer herself conceives it. In what follows we will come at this issue in a rather more statistical way.

Chapter Five

Who Finds It Easiest to Foster?

Introduction

In our last chapter we tried to convey the feel of fostering as related to us by what foster carers wrote. In the rest of the book we take a more statistical approach. In this chapter we introduce three different measures of how the carers reacted to fostering. We then explore how these measures varied with the characteristics of carers discussed in Chapter 2.

Our three measures were the 'satisfaction with fostering' ('fostering score' for short), the *General Health Questionnaire* (GHQ) (which we used as a measure of personal strain – 'strain score'), and 'intention to leave' (whether or not the carer intended to leave over the next two years).

Satisfaction with fostering

The fostering score was made up of nine variables,[1] themselves derived from our reading of the literature and our plot studies with a group of foster carers. The variables covered the foster carers' assessment of:

- the impact of fostering on housing
- the impact of fostering on leisure
- the impact of fostering on finance
- the impact of fostering on employment
- the impact of fostering on family relationships
- the impact of fostering on individual members of the family
- whether they got a lot of satisfaction from fostering

- whether they felt fostering enriched their lives
- whether 'everyone in family pleased' that they fostered.

The reliability of the resulting score was satisfactory (alpha = 0.80) and the score itself was approximately normally distributed (an important consideration when developing a measure such as this).

Strain score

Foster carers were asked to complete a shortened (12 item) version of the GHQ as a measure of sense of well-being. This was devised as a screening device identifying those who, on further investigation by a psychiatrist, would have a high probability of receiving a psychiatric diagnosis. The 'strain score' was also normally distributed. The questionnaire included some 'positive' questions – for example, 'Have you recently felt you were playing a useful part in things?' – and also 'negative' ones – for example, 'Have you recently lost much sleep over worry?'[2]

On this measure 55 per cent of the respondents were experiencing no symptoms of strain whatever. Only 17 per cent were experiencing as many as three symptoms or more. (For comparison, Farmer and her colleagues [2002] found that just under a quarter scored in the 'clinical or sub-clinical' range of the same instrument.) As we will see later some of those experiencing strain were doing so because of events such as bereavements unrelated to fostering. For this reason we asked the foster carers whether the way they had answered the questions had anything to do with the fact that they had been fostering. Only 31 per cent said that it had and not all of these felt that the impact of fostering had been negative. Overall, only around 12 per cent of the sample reported three or more symptoms and said that the way they had been feeling had to do with their being foster carers.

Intention to leave

Our final variable was 'intention to leave'. As we have seen, when asked whether they might leave within the next two years, 7 per cent said that they definitely would, 32 per cent that they might do, and 61 per cent that they definitely would not.

Associations between our three measures

As might be expected, the three variables were associated with each other although the associations were not particularly strong.[3] It is possible to wish to leave fostering for reasons other than being under strain or perceiving it negatively. Similarly it is possible for foster carers to be under strain for reasons that have nothing to do with fostering. For these reasons we have not combined these variables into a single score.

Carer characteristics: attitudes to fostering and strain

In this section we explore the relationship between our three 'outcome variables' and the personal and family situation of the carer. Our 'independent variables' (those we use to try and explain our outcomes) include the sex of the foster carer, and their age, ethnicity, family composition and educational level.

Sex of main carer

We had no hypotheses on the relationship between our measures of attitude and stress on the one hand and the sex of the carer on the other and we found none.

Age of carer

Previous research (Soothill and Derbyshire 1982) has suggested that some foster carers feel that it is time to 'retire'. As we saw in the last chapter, a number of foster carers explained their intention to do so over the next two years on the grounds that they felt they were now too old to carry on. Some, in addition, felt that they would see out a particular foster child but that they lacked the energy to start again.

For these reasons, we expected that foster carers who were aged 60 or over would be more likely to intend to give up fostering, even though they would not necessarily be under greater stress or more negative to fostering than others. By contrast, we expected that younger foster carers (those aged 30 or less) would be likely to find fostering more stressful, partly because they would be less experienced, and partly because they would have other competing responsibilities in terms of young children of their own.

There was some evidence for these hypotheses. Older carers were the least stressed group – 52 per cent of them were in the lowest third of the GHQ score. Young carers (under 29s) were the group apparently under the most strain. The differences between the three groups on this measure of strain were unlikely to occur by chance, but were not large.

The differences between the groups on our 'fostering score' were larger and clearer. We divided the scores on this measure into three equal groups that we called 'positive', 'mixed' and 'negative'. Fifty-six per cent of the older carers but only 16 per cent of the younger ones had positive scores. At the other end of the scale, 44 per cent of the younger carers had negative scores, as against 24 per cent of the older carers. So in general, the older the carer, the more favourable their attitudes were likely to be.

The situation was very different when it came to intentions to leave. One in five of the older carers said they intended to do so within the next two years. Only 1 in 20 of the middle group of carers and none of the younger carers said this.

Family composition

A variety of aspects of family composition might be expected to affect the main carer's experience of fostering. These include the presence of other adults, whether the carer has had children, whether these children are present in the family and the difference in age between the children and the foster children.

Our main hypotheses were that the main carer would be under less strain and/or have more favourable attitudes to fostering in families:

- where there was an adult couple (since the stresses could be shared)
- in families with no children (since there would be less competition and the carers would be more likely to have chosen to foster as they liked children rather than because it fitted their family situation).

Our hypotheses on the effects of other adults were not borne out. Quite the reverse – in families where there was a couple, the carer tended to express slightly more negative attitudes to fostering ($p<0.05$).

Families with no birth children in the house also did not differ from others in the way expected.

Work

Full-time or part-time work could have a variety of effects on attitudes to fostering and levels of strain.

In general, we thought that there might be a difference between 'family-oriented' and 'work-oriented' foster carers. The former might want to look after children even if it meant not going out to work. They would be less likely than the others to work and more likely to have favourable attitudes to fostering. The work-oriented carers would not wish to look after children if it got in the way of work. They would be particularly unhappy with fostering if it did so.

In relation to strain, predictions were difficult to make. On the one hand, going out to work could reduce strain – providing additional money, a break from the strains of caring and new sources of support and self-esteem. On the other hand, there could be additional strain arising from competition between responsibilities at work and home.

As predicted, foster carers who did not work were more likely to score positively on our overall measure of attitudes to fostering. They were significantly less likely to say that they were going to leave in the next two years, or that they might do so; they were more positive about the effects on their families and about foster care itself.

Table 5.1 illustrates these findings. As can be seen, the differences, while very unlikely to occur by chance, were not spectacular. The group most likely to have definite intentions to leave were those who had full-time work. Those who had part-time work were not so definite. They were, however, the group most likely to consider the *possibility* of stopping. Forty-four per cent of them said they might not stay in fostering, whereas the comparable percentage for those with no work was 29 per cent.

Table 5.1 Whether main carer working and attitudes to fostering			
Whether working	*n*	**Intends to leave[a] (%)**	**Favourable to foster care[b] (%)**
Yes: full-time	156	11	43
Yes: part-time	240	5	41
No	492	6	54
Total	888	7	49

Source: General Questionnaire.
[a] Chi square = 29.82, df = 4, $p<0.001$ (df reflects inclusion of 'may stop' as category).
[b] Chi square = 13.07, df = 2, $p<0.001$ (defined as above the median for fostering score).

Again as predicted, those who stated that they would have liked to have worked more, and felt they would have done so but for fostering, were particularly negative. Moreover, those who felt prevented from working more by fostering expressed, in comparison with others, a high level of strain ($p<0.0001$).

In contrast to the situation over attitudes to fostering, there was no clear relationship between strain and whether a carer worked full-time, part-time or not at all. There was, however, a relationship among those who said that the way they answered the GHQ questions had to do with the fact that they fostered. They were more stressed if they worked, and particularly so if they worked part-time ($p<0.01$).

So it seems likely that the impact of fostering on mental health is dependent on the aspirations and perceptions of the carer. Those who want to go out to work, and attribute their inability to do so to fostering, are stressed. Those who do not want to go out to work, or who attribute their lack of work to other causes, find their life and fostering easier.

Housing

As noted in Chapter 2, we asked whether foster children and members of the family were all able to have a bedroom for themselves. We expected that carers in families where this was not so would express more strain and more negative attitudes to fostering. We thought that this would be even more so if this lack of space was attributed to fostering.

As it turned out, there was no evidence that a comparative lack of bedrooms was associated with a high degree of strain on the part of the carer. Nor was there any clear relationship between our other measures of attitudes and the amount of space as assessed on these measures. Nor were carers in houses where room was short more likely to say that they intended to leave over the next two years.

Clearly the amount of space available for foster children and families is an important issue. However, on these data it does not have a major impact on those carers who foster.

Ethnicity

There was no *a priori* reason for thinking that those from ethnic backgrounds other than British would differ from others.

In practice, neither group was more likely than the other to say that they would stop fostering in the next two years. However, minority ethnic carers expressed significantly less strain ($p<0.01$). At first sight, there seems to be no obvious reason why this should be so. It may reflect cultural differences in the way the questionnaire was filled in, or be a chance finding, or reflect some important distinction between the two groups. A possible explanation for it is given in Chapter 6.

Educational level

We had no hypotheses on the effect of educational level on foster carer strain or attitudes. As it turned out, the higher the educational level of the foster carer, the lower the level of expressed strain ($p<0.01$). It seems likely that this finding arises from the connection between class and educational level – the more highly educated foster carers were probably better off and experienced lower levels of strain for this reason – rather than because they found fostering particularly easy.

The only relationship between attitudes and educational level was at a more detailed level. Those of a higher educational level were more likely to see fostering as having a negative impact on their social arrangements. Conversely, the less educated were significantly more likely to see the arrangements as having a positive impact. There were similar contrasting trends in relation to finance, employment and housing (the latter possibly because fostering had enabled those in council housing to move).

So it seems likely that the impact of fostering on carers' standards of living can be comparatively beneficial (or at least not harmful) when they have a weak position in the job market, but not when they have a potentially strong one. The more highly educated foster carers have a wider range of well-paid opportunities available to them. Hence they see themselves as more disadvantaged by foster care.

Kinds of fostering undertaken

We had five broad hypotheses on the effects of different kinds of fostering on foster carers. These related to:

- Experience – we expected experienced foster carers to be less stressed and more committed to foster care than inexperienced ones.

- Age of foster children – we expected foster carers looking after older children to score 'worse' on these variables than those looking after younger ones.

- Difference in ages of children and foster children – we expected that carers would express more negative attitudes to fostering when there was little difference in age between their resident children and their foster children.

- Expectations – we expected foster carers who had fostered children for whom they were not approved, or whom they preferred not to take, to do 'worse' on these variables than other foster carers.

- Role clarity – foster carers with more clearly defined roles were expected to do better on these variables than others with less clearly defined roles.

Our hypotheses on age and experience were derived from the literature on foster care disruptions (see, for example, Berridge 1997). We simply expected the variables that have been associated with foster care disruptions to be associated with foster carer attitudes and stress. Our hypotheses on expectations and clarity were *a priori*. It seemed to us likely that foster carers who took the kind of children they wanted, and were clear about what they were expected to do, would find their work easier.

In addition, we explored the relationship between the sex and number of the foster children and our measures. This was more because these seemed key features of foster care than because we had any definite hypotheses about them.

We first tested our hypotheses by seeing if the variables were associated in the way we predicted. We then checked some of the more obvious confounding variables. (A confounding variable may explain an association between two others because it is itself associated with both of them.) So we looked for example at whether the relationship between experience and attitudes was affected by an association between both of these variables and the age of the foster children.

Experience

We considered two measures of experience – the number of foster children previously taken and the number of years involved in fostering. We divided each of these into three roughly equal groups representing 'low experience', 'medium experience' and 'considerable experience'.

Neither of our measures of experience were strongly associated with the strain score (a small positive association between years of fostering and strain was explained by the fact that the more experienced foster carers had older foster children).

There was a weak, and barely significant, association between our fostering score and years of experience – a consequence, perhaps, of the fact that those with positive attitudes were more likely to continue.

Somewhat disturbingly, those with more years' experience were more likely to be contemplating leaving foster care. This association remained after we had taken account of the greater age of the more experienced carers. The explanation is uncertain. It could be a chance finding. It may reflect 'burn-out', the lure of better support and remuneration on offer in the independent sector or discontent with new fashions in foster care. It may reflect the fact that, for some, foster care is a choice for a particular stage in life (e.g. when the carer has young children) and is relinquished when this life stage passes.

Age of foster children

In testing our hypotheses about the impact of age, we looked at the average age of the foster children in the household.

At first sight the results were reasonably clear-cut. The greater the average age of the children, the more negative the attitudes of carers to fostering. More specifically, foster carers with older children were more likely to say that they had thoughts of leaving, that they intended to do so in the next two years, that the impact of fostering on their family was negative and that they did not enjoy it.

More detailed examination (see Table 5.2) showed a rather more complicated pattern. The quarter of foster carers who had the oldest children contained half those who were definitely intending to stop fostering. However, the least favourable attitudes to fostering were found in the quartile just below them, and the most favourable attitudes among those with the youngest foster children. Presumably, the group with the oldest children expect them to leave in the near future and so are more likely to be thinking of leaving themselves. The group with the next oldest children may have, on average, more difficult children and are less favourable to foster care on that account.

Our measure of strain was only associated with average age of foster child if the foster carer attributed the strain to fostering. In these instances the association was highly significant.

Table 5.2 Ages of foster children and intentions and attitudes of carers			
Average age of foster children	n	Intends to leave[a] (%)	Favourable to foster care[b] (%)
Lowest quartile	187	3	60
2nd quartile	203	4	49
3rd quartile	171	4	42
Highest quartile	207	10	49
Total	768	5	50

Source: General Questionnaire.

Note: Table restricted to carers who were fostering.

[a] Chi square = 16.00, df = 6, p = 0.014 (df reflect inclusion of 'might stop' as a category).

[b] Chi square = 12.48, df = 3, p = 0.006.

Differences in age between foster children and birth children

We had expected that a small difference in the average age of foster children and birth children would be associated with more negative attitudes to fostering. In practice, the age difference between two groups of children was related to attitudes to fostering but not in the way we predicted.

We computed a measure of age difference between foster and birth children by subtracting the average age of the former from that of the latter. Among those who had children of their own in the house, attitudes were much more positive where the children were older than the foster children or when there was not much difference in age. Attitudes were more likely to be negative when the birth children were younger than the foster children.

This finding could have various explanations. A natural explanation would be that older foster children are more difficult and it is this, rather than the resulting age difference, that produces the problem. However, an analysis that took account of the age of the foster children suggested that this was not the reason. It could be that older birth children are less likely to feel in competition with younger foster children and more likely to be helpful over their care. Again, however, an analysis that took the average age of the carers' children into account suggested that this was not the whole explanation (it may be some of it).

A possible explanation is that carers feel that children who are older than their own exploit them or dominate them. Triseliotis and his colleagues (2000) report that some carers were reluctant to take older children for this reason. We have, however, no direct evidence for this in our research.

Numbers of foster children

In general, the greater the number of foster children in the house, the lower the likelihood that the carer was thinking of leaving foster care in the next two years. The proportions definitely intending to stay rose from 57 per cent where there was only one child, to 78 per cent where there were three, falling slightly after that among the small number of households where there were four or five foster children.

Table 5.3 Number of foster children by intention to stop fostering over the next two years				
Number of foster children	*n*	Yes (%)	Not sure (%)	No (%)
1	365	7	36	57
2	242	4	26	70
3	109	1	21	78
4	35	6	26	68
5	17	–	41	59
Total	768	5	30	65

Source: General Questionnaire.
Note: Table applies to those with foster children.
Chi square = 24.52, df = 8, $p = 0.002$.

The number of foster children was not strongly associated with either our measure of strain or attitudes to fostering. So the likely explanation lies in the commitment of foster carers. Where they intend to leave, they may be less willing to take on new children. Where they have a number of children, they are less likely to have a natural break where they can cease caring in the near future.

Expectations

We asked foster carers a series of questions about the kinds of children they preferred to foster and, by contrast, the kinds they would rather not foster.

The proportions that responded to these questions varied from 66 per cent to 77 per cent. Among the carers who answered, the strongest opinions were about teenagers. A third of the sample expressed a preference for them while 40 per cent would rather not have fostered them. These preferences seem to have carried weight with those making the placements. The average of the foster children varied from over 14 where the foster carers preferred them, through ten when they were indifferent to just over six when they preferred not to have them. There was a similar trend in the reverse direction for those who preferred babies or toddlers.

However, although foster carer preferences seem to have been generally followed, this was not invariably the case. We expected that where the ages of children in the house did not match the expressed preferences of the foster carer, this would be reflected in greater strain and lower satisfaction. Conversely, those caring for foster children in an age group they preferred should be more content.

As a test of this hypothesis we compared the foster carer preferences with a list of the kind of cases whom they said they had fostered. Overall, 30 per cent of the carers reported fostering children of a kind they preferred not to take. As we predicted, these carers were slightly more likely to express negative attitudes to fostering. However, the differences were slight and barely significant.

Role clarity

As described above, we believed that greater role clarity would be associated with greater satisfaction and lower strain. We tested this idea indirectly by identifying situations in which role clarity seemed likely and seeing whether foster carers in these situations had lower levels of strain.

The situations we examined were:

- foster carer works for an agency
- foster carer reports being on a special project
- foster carer does not have more than one approved role
- average time of foster children in placement matches approved role.

Only one of these hypotheses received any support. Carers who reported that they were, or thought they might be, on a special scheme had significantly better scores on our overall measure of attitudes to fostering ($p<0.05$). The difference, however, was not spectacular.

Sex of foster children

We found no association between the sex of the foster children and our measures of strain and attitudes to fostering. This is not, of course, to say that the sex of the child is unimportant in fostering – only that from this point of view, and on average, female and male foster children can be equally easy or difficult.

Conclusions

In some ways, the most striking feature of this chapter lies in the lack of strong associations rather than their presence. One reason for this will become apparent in the next chapter. People's reactions to fostering depend heavily on what happens when they foster. Relatively stable features of their situation – the number of their own children and their own involvement in work – may be much less influential in how they felt about fostering than their experience of foster children who turn out well, or of breakdowns and accusations of abuse.

A second reason for the lack of strong associations with our chosen measures is that foster carers, like the rest of the population, are affected by stresses that have nothing to do with fostering. Many of those who appeared to be under strain did not attribute this to the fact they fostered. The most natural explanation for the association between educational level and low levels of strain lies in the probable prosperity of more highly educated carers.

That said, there was some evidence that the stress, or lack of it, in fostering is related to how the carer sees other aspects of their lives – particularly work. Foster carers who wanted to work more, and attributed their inability to do so to fostering, were particularly stressed. Similarly, foster carers who did work were in certain respects less committed to fostering than those who did not.

Fostering also has to be seen in relation to stages of life and to other opportunities. Older foster carers were more likely to feel that it was time to 'retire'. Relatively young foster carers were more likely to plan on continuing, but were under somewhat greater strain. Carers with a higher standard of education were more likely to see fostering as having a negative impact on various aspects of their lives.

These findings may have as much relevance to the recruitment of carers as they do to their retention. As we will see later, people leave foster care at least as much because of what happens to them as because of plans relating to their family situation. However, the factors they weigh up when planning their future are likely to be those they consider when deciding whether to foster in the first place. So an ability to appeal to carers who want to work, as well as to those who do not, may well be a crucial element in attempts to increase the number of people who apply to foster as well as to attempts to retain them.

Notes

1. Each impact variable was scored between 1 (positive impact) and 3 (negative impact) with 2 representing a mixed or neutral impact. The remaining questions were scored between 1 (positive) and 4 (negative) according to the strength of their agreement that fostering was a positive experience. In order to ensure that each item contributed a roughly equal amount to the total score, we transformed them so that each had as far as possible a mean of 0 and a standard deviation of 1.

2. Two methods of scoring are available. One counts the number of times a respondent says 'less or much less than usual' for the positive questions and 'more or much more than usual' for the negative questions. The other method scores the positive questions in the same way but counts 'same as usual' as well as 'more or much more than usual' for the negative ones. The second gives a more normal distribution, and we preferred it for this reason (see Bowling 1991; Goldberg and Williams 1988).

3. The correlations were very highly significant but never larger than 0.31 (between strain and attitude to fostering).

Chapter Six

Stressful 'Events' for Foster Carers

Introduction

So far we have been looking at the relatively 'fixed' aspects of foster carers – their ages, the number of children they have, whether they work, and so on. We turn now to the things that happen in foster care, and in particular to 'stressful events' or experiences which are neither planned nor predicted. As we will see, these appear to have a powerful impact on how foster care is experienced.[1]

Stressful events

The difficult experiences, or 'events', we have in mind are those such as allegations of abuse, or fostering disruptions, which constitute a definite and serious episode in a carer's fostering career. Most of these build up over a period, so that the word 'event' is not intended to imply too rigid a boundary in time. Moreover, 'events' are clearly not the sole causes of stress in foster care. As we have seen, daily 'hassles' – the unfriendly comments of neighbours, the problems of transporting different children to different places, the need to provide reports, and numerous other undramatic but wearing experiences – may also place a strain on the foster carer. Nevertheless, there are a number of more clear-cut 'events' or episodes that might be expected to have a considerable impact. So it is important to explore how common they are, what they mean to foster carers and what their consequences seem to be.

Our research covered six 'events' in particular. These were selected on the basis of the existing literature, which has highlighted certain kinds of difficulties as having a notably discouraging impact on the foster carers who experience them. The literature is particularly concerned with disruptions and allegations, and hence with the relationship between foster carer and child. However, relationships between the foster carer and the social services department, those within the foster family, and those between the foster family and the birth family are also important (see Berridge 1997; Sellick and Thoburn 1996). We therefore included 'events' which would be likely to affect all these relationships and which might for this reason have an impact on the foster carer's mental health (by which we mean sense of well-being rather than psychiatric status) and attitude to fostering. We list the six 'events' below, together with the reasons for selecting them.

Breakdowns or disruptions

These were defined by Berridge and Cleaver (1987) as 'a placement ending that was not included in the social work plan either in the ending itself or the timing of the termination'. A major concern about foster care has been the instability of many of the placements. Qualitative work by Aldgate and Hawley (1986) suggests that these are often highly stressful for carers and children alike.

Allegations

It has been suggested that roughly one in six foster carers will experience a complaint or an allegation in the course of their fostering career (Wheal 1995). The fear of allegations puts restrictions on carers' lives – for example, they may take steps to ensure male carers are never alone with female foster children. Farmer and her colleagues (2002) found that around half the carers in their study confessed to background worries of this kind. There is evidence that the incidence of complaints is growing (Coffin 1993), and the greater public awareness of child abuse and, arguably, the greater attention to what parents and children are saying would seem to increase the likelihood of allegations being made. Triseliotis and his colleagues (2000) report an incidence of 3.5 allegations per 100 carers per year in Scotland, only 16 per cent of which resulted in compulsory registration, a finding which suggests that over an average of fostering career of just over seven years, around one in five carers would experience an unconfirmed allegation. There is evidence that foster carers find the experience and the accompanying investigations highly distressing (Hicks and Nixon 1989).

Relationship with birth parents

As discussed in our introduction early research suggested that foster carers often had little contact with birth parents and that such contacts as they had were rarely sources of difficulty to them (Berridge and Cleaver 1987; Rowe *et al.* 1984). Indeed, concern about the lack of involvement and contact between birth parents and their 'looked-after' children had a major influence on the Children Act 1989, and to the emphasis on working in partnership in the guidance accompanying the legislation (Department of Health 1991a) and in *Working Together* (Department of Health 1991b). Both our own subsequent work, reported in our next book, and that of others (e.g. Cleaver 2000) suggest that the frequency of contacts between birth parents and foster children has greatly increased since the earlier studies. The carers rarely see these contacts as problem free (Cleaver 2000). Others have found that a sizeable proportion of these contacts are stressful for carers (Farmer *et al.* 2002; Triseliotis *et al.* 2000), a finding strongly supported by the findings reported below and in our next book.

Family tensions

The extent and persistence of difficult behaviour among foster children, and the adverse effects which fostering may in consequence have on foster families, have been described in a number of studies (Aldgate and Hawley 1986; Baxter 1989). One of the recurring and best validated findings of foster care research is that breakdown is more likely where the foster carers are looking after their own children as well as foster children (see, for example, Berridge 1997; Thoburn 1996). It seems likely that the reason has to do with family tensions, and conceivable that these may also involve spouses. Thoburn, Murdoch and O'Brien (1986) list a strong marriage or partnership as a factor leading to successful foster care, and Aldgate and Hawley (1986) mention marital disagreements as being sometimes part of the build-up to a fostering disruption.

'Tug of love' cases

Disagreements with social services departments over where children should live make the headlines in national newspapers. They have not been the subject of research, although Berridge and Cleaver (1987) mention them as part of the background to disruptions. They can be seen, perhaps, as the most dramatic example of the tensions that arise between the expectations of social services that foster carers do not compete with birth parents when the latter wish to resume care, and the feeling that foster carers may naturally have for the children. As such, they are likely to be highly stressful.

Other disagreements with social services

It seems reasonable to suppose that as the task of fostering becomes more complex and more fraught (a likely result of the changes introduced by the Children Act 1989) the relationships between foster carers and social workers will become even more vital to the process, but also more prone to tension and disagreement. Social services may disagree with foster carers over a wide range of issues – for example, over the way the carers discipline or bring up the foster child. Such disagreements may involve matters that are central to the foster carers' definition of themselves as caring and competent people and, potentially, might be seen as highly stressful. Again, they do not seem to have been the subject of research.

As will be seen from the above, varying amounts are known about these various 'events', and that which is known may or may not now apply as the legislation and guidance have moved things on. The immediate objectives of this chapter are to address this problem in three ways. First, we describe the frequency with which our sample of foster carers have experienced these problems in the course of their fostering career and, as a subsidiary objective, the degree to which this frequency varies with length of time spent fostering and type of foster care provided. Second, we try to say something about the nature of these experiences by describing them in the foster carers' own words. Third, we examine their impact by looking at their association with a measure of strain, with the foster carers' satisfaction with fostering, and with their intention to carry on with fostering.

How many foster carers had experienced an 'event'?

The foster carers were asked whether they had experienced a number of 'special difficulties' since they began fostering. Table 6.1 gives the proportion that responded in each category.

As can be seen, the most common event (experienced by nearly half the carers) was a breakdown or disruption. In addition, nearly a third said they had experienced severe family tensions because of a difficult foster placement, and nearly a quarter said that they had had severe difficulties with birth parents. At the other end of the scale, removal of a foster child against their strong advice was reported by less than one in seven.

Table 6.1 Proportion of foster carers reporting 'events'

Have previously experienced	n	% of total
Breakdown or disruption of placement	439	47
Allegation by child (e.g. of abuse)	149	16
Severe difficulties with birth parents	229	24
Severe family tensions because of difficult foster placement	290	31
Removal of foster child against your strong advice	125	13
Other strong disagreement with social services over plans for child	182	19
At least one of above	617	65
Total	944	

Source: General Questionnaire.
Note: As some foster carers had experienced more than one 'event', the total is greater than 100%.

Table 6.2 Proportion of foster carers reporting at least one 'event' by time fostering

Time fostering	n	% of total
Less than 1 year	114	30
1–2 years	101	47
3–5 years	203	72
6–11 years	264	74
12 years and more	188	81
Total	870	66

Source: General Questionnaire.
Chi square = 112.24, df = 1, $p<0.00001$.

The likelihood of an event naturally increases with the number of foster placements and the length of time during which a respondent has been fostering. The relevant data are set out in Table 6.2.

It is striking that almost exactly a third of those who had been fostering for a year or less had already experienced at least one event. The likelihood that those who have not previously experienced an event will experience one in a subsequent year must be somewhat less than this (otherwise at least 80% would have experienced an event within four years). Nevertheless, more than three-quarters of foster carers with five or more years' experience had had at least one of these upsetting experiences. In a similar way, the likelihood that a foster carer would experience at least one 'event' increased from 42 per cent among those who had fostered no more than four children to 82 per cent among those who had fostered 15 or more.

As can be seen from Tables 6.3 and 6.4, the likelihood that a foster carer would have experienced an event varied with the type of foster care provided.

These differences were very unlikely to have occurred by chance. However, a number of them were explained by association between the type of foster care and the length of time for which the foster carer had been caring, and the number of foster children they had taken. Relatives, for example, had typically been caring for a shorter time and taken fewer children than other foster carers. If these differences are taken into account relatives do not 'do better' than others.[2]

Table 6.3 Mainstream, relative and respite carers by experience of 'events'

Type of carer	n	No 'event' (%)	At least one 'event' (%)
Relative carer only	59	66	34
Respite carer only	290	41	59
Both relative and respite carer	13	62	38
Neither relative nor respite carer	589	28	72
Total	951	49	51

Source: General Questionnaire.
Chi square = 45.66, df = 3, $p < 0.00001$.

Table 6.4 Age of oldest foster child by experience of 'event'			
Age of oldest foster child	n	No 'event' (%)	At least one 'event' (%)
Under 5	107	50	50
5–10	205	42	58
11 and over	455	27	73
Total	767	34	66

Source: General Questionnaire.
Chi square = 29.32, df = 2, $p<0.00001$.

The meaning of 'events'

We placed these 'events' in context by asking the foster carers to comment on their experience of them. We first 'trawled' all the questionnaires where an event was ticked in order to gain an understanding of what was involved, identified the main themes, and selected quotations that seemed to represent them. The replies made it clear that one event often involved others. For example, a difficult foster child might lead both to family tensions and to a disruption. The multi-faceted nature of many 'events' is brought out by the quotations given below. In grouping the quotations, we have followed the classification that the carers implied by their ticks on our questionnaire (e.g. if they ticked 'disruption' but included a description of family tensions, we have reported this under the head of 'disruption').

Placement breakdown

The comments on *placement breakdown* support Aldgate and Hawley's study (1986) in suggesting that the impact is both distressing to the carer in itself and also because it is often the culmination of a long series of stressful 'events'. An experienced carer from one of the unitary authorities who had suffered four of these disruptions described her sense of failure thus:

Hate breakdowns. I feel a failure. Could I have offered more?

This may be compounded by a sense of isolation from other sources of support or ameliorated by their presence. The carer just quoted had experienced both:

> We had a girl who just kept packing and finally ran off. We felt we did not have any support from social services until afterwards. Our link worker did come out straight away to reassure us as it comes as a shock.

Many of the comments convey the severity of the difficulties before the disruption and the feelings on the part of the carers of being stretched to breaking point before they have given up:

> I have had two boys who had behavioural difficulties which affected own grandchildren. We stood it all we could before we made the hard choice of having them removed.

> Daily reports were given via telephone. One child became uncontrollable, verbally aggressive, not returning home and eventually I was kicked and punched in the face, this caused final breakdown.

Allegations

As indicated in our introduction, earlier research has indicated that allegations of abuse are not an uncommon experience for foster carers. The approximate numbers in our sample (138 or 16% of the total) were in keeping with the experience of the NFCA (National Foster Care Association), but were heavily concentrated on allegations of physical abuse. It is unlikely that the only allegations were of this nature, and foster carers, even when exonerated, may have felt inhibited about describing allegations of sexual abuse:

> I was accused of hitting a child which later at a meeting she confessed that she was lying. I felt that I did not get hardly any support.

> Alleged to have smacked the younger child age two. The three-year-old reported it. It was found untrue. Luckily I had taken them to the doctor's and he knew about the bruises so he could say I had not done it.

The overwhelming impression from the comments is that it was not so much the allegation itself, or the fact that social services had to investigate it, that was the worst aspect of the experience. Rather, it was the lack of information and exclusion from the proceedings, and poor feedback concerning the conclusion, that really seemed to rankle. Obviously, it is extremely difficult to make such enquiries sensitively and, even if foster carers are kept informed, they may not find the situation very much more tolerable. Nevertheless, carers in our study felt that the pain could be reduced. One single female carer described her feelings about the way in which the allegation was handled thus:

> An allegation of physical abuse was made against me by a so-called professional. The allegation was totally unfounded and was probably self-inflicted by the child itself. I cannot describe the effect that such an allegation had on myself and my daughter. Whilst I accept that allegations must be taken seriously, I feel that official procedures were not followed in my case and I was left in the dark as to what was happening. No support was offered at all.

Difficulties with birth parents

Difficulties with birth parents are obviously not confined to fostering by relatives and, as we have seen, roughly a quarter of the carers reported them. Some of these difficulties had to do with handling aggressive or violent birth parents:

> Mother and current boy friend attended contact. Boy friend always drunk. Mother argumentative/aggressive, threatening.

> We have experienced threats of serious physical violence against us and this child from natural parents with previous convictions of serious violence including murder... In these circumstances where it is known that there is past serious violence we don't think it appropriate for natural families to know the name or address of the people caring for the child.

Such experiences could lead placements to disrupt:

> I have had four children removed for the same reason – violence [of birth parents] towards us.

A second common cause of complaint arose from the impact of the birth parents on the child:

> Two years ago we had a problem with a third foster child (boy). He was 12 years and had been with us two years. In that time we found because of very little access to his birth parents he was settled and happy. Until the SSD [social services department] decided to allow him access to his

parents' own home without our knowledge. He became aggressive and abusive towards myself and our other foster child.

Many of the children are far more disruptive after contact with birth parents.

Sometimes the birth parents were seen as deliberately working against the foster carer:

Brain washing the child that we are bad foster parents.

Encouraged child to be naughty.

There were also complaints that social services gave precedence to the needs of the parents over those of the child:

It seems that contact is agreed at weekends too readily and can be very disruptive to the child because they feel left out of things and it can stop certain things for the family.

Social services are biased in favour of natural parents, however much damage they do their own children.

Family tensions

We have already in Chapter 4 said something about the impact of fostering on the family. Understandably, *severe family tensions* often led to the final breakdown of the placement. An experienced foster carer from one of the shire counties felt that her family had suffered as a result of the inappropriate placing with them of two very difficult children:

We had a troubled placement with two siblings who had been sexually abused. They were seriously disturbed and disruptive and badly affected our own children. We were not warned of any history of abuse or of the children's behaviour. It was a great strain on our family and we asked to have the children moved after four weeks.

The family tensions that may arise in dealing with a difficult foster placement are clearly considerable and the comments offered described a whole range of such stresses. In one case, for example, it seems as if the carer chose fostering over her marriage:

Fostering contributed to the breakdown of my marriage because fostering has become a way of life.

Other problems reflect the wear and tear of dealing with difficult foster children or the distress felt by other members of the family at the effect on the main foster carer:

> Tension caused mainly by lack of sleep and screaming of child.

> Sometimes my son and daughter get annoyed at the way [the foster children] treat me. This causes difficulty.

Although placements with relatives are often sought because they may be less disruptive for the child – a view supported by research (Berridge and Cleaver 1987; Rowe *et al.* 1984) and guidance (Department of Health 1991b) – some comments show that they are not immune to difficulties and may carry some particular stresses:

> I feel under lots of pressure because of the girls' parents. Basically because they are my family and it's hard to tell them how they make me feel.

> When my cousin whose children I'm fostering started making things difficult by being abusive the social worker did everything in resolving the problem by finding another contact place.

(See Appendix 3 and Sykes *et al.* 2002 for further discussion of our findings around the difficulties of relative carers.)

Removal of child against carer's advice

We also asked about times when a foster child had be *moved against the carer's strong advice*. Such 'events' were clearly a source of distress. The foster carers commented that plans for rehabilitation were adhered to, come what may, that children were returned to environments which had caused the trouble in the first place, and that their judgement had been vindicated by subsequent 'events':

> Father's behaviour was wrong with children and myself and social worker wanted children to stay in care but they still went home.

> On advice of 'guardian ad litem', girls were placed with aunty to live, hence in my opinion back in family unit whence they had been taken because of problems.

> Foster children went back to their natural parents. Within six weeks they were both back in care. We strongly disagreed with the social workers

and said the placement would break down which it did and the children lost a placement with us.

Sometimes the removal was designed to relieve the pressure on the foster carer. One, for example, was given another placement because of the foster carer's serious illness. Nonetheless, the foster carer felt that the child's need for a stable placement should have been given greater weight. She commented that her own children had remained with her, and went on:

> The middle child was placed in another foster home against our wishes and against advice. He eventually returned but he had learned a whole new way of life and I don't think he ever recovered.

A number of these conflicts seemed to involve issues around race. One white carer from one of the unitary authorities commented:

> One child we had was a quarter Asian and her mother wanted her to be placed with a white family. After six months with us it was decided she should go to a half Asian family. We were not at all happy with this as the child was very settled.

Another carer, also white, and this time from one of the London boroughs, also felt that issues of race had taken undue precedence over consideration of the child's other needs:

> Black child moved to black placement. No consideration given to child's feeling when he wanted to stay.

Other strong disagreements

Finally, we asked parents about *other strong disagreements with social services*. The replies sometimes conveyed a feeling that they were not given appropriate status:

> Foster carers are second class citizens.

> Foster carers are unimportant and their views are ignored.

Other comments focused more specifically on the way in which decisions were taken:

> After a placement breakdown, foster carers are shut out of planning. Continually upset by the children's social workers. Plans do not accord with day-to-day experience of actual child.

A number of comments focused on resources supplementary to the placement (e.g. psychiatric resources) or to lack of appropriate placements, so that children had to stay longer than originally agreed, or go to an inappropriate placement:

> Any difficulties we have experienced have usually arisen because child's social worker has tried to pressure us into extending placement after the agreed terms, even when the placement has been less than ideal match.

Carers' feelings about themselves and about fostering

Given the traumatic nature of some of the 'events' described above, it seemed important to see whether they were associated with our measure of strain exhibited by the carers and with their attitude to continuing fostering. We examined whether those who had experienced the 'events' discussed earlier were more likely to show signs of being under strain than those who had not. Table 6.5 sets out the results.

For the statistically minded, two 'events' (allegations and experience of removal) were not significantly associated with strain, as tested by analysis of variance and reported in Table 6.5. However, they were significantly associated with it if a rather more sensitive analysis was used to compare the average score for those with an event with the average score for those without one (allegations, $t = 1.99$, df $= 942$, $p = 0.047$; contested removal [unequal variances], $t = 2.14$, df $= 152.74$, $p = 0.034$). The remaining 'events' were all associated with strain at a high level of significance.

We next examined the association between 'events' and attitudes to fostering. All the 'events' except experience of allegations were significantly associated with less positive attitudes towards foster care. The associations with breakdowns and negative impacts on the family were particularly strong.

As can be seen in Table 6.6 all 'events', except for the removal of a child against advice, were significantly associated with the frequency with which a carer had thought of giving up fostering. Taken together, the results for this question suggest that about 60 per cent of our respondents had considered giving up fostering at some time in the past, a finding broadly in line with Gorin's (1997) study. Similarly Triseliotis and his colleagues (2000) report that around half their sample of Scottish carers had sometimes (38%) or often (10%) thought of giving up in the past.

Future intentions were less closely associated with the existence of 'events', and only in the case of family tensions was the association significant.

Table 6.5 Experience of 'events' and symptoms of strain

| Type of 'event' | n | Degree of strain (%) | | | Prob. of difference |
		Low	Medium	High	
Breakdown/ disruption					Chi sq = 9.57
Yes	439	23	36	41	df = 1
No	505	30	39	31	p = 0.002
Allegation					Chi sq = 2.01
Yes	149	27	37	36	df = 1
No	795	22	38	40	p = 0.1559
Severe difficulties with birth parents					Chi sq = 15.49
Yes	229	20	32	48	df = 1
No	715	28	38	33	p = 0.00008
Severe family tensions					Chi sq = 23.33
Yes	290	18	37	45	df = 1
No	654	30	38	32	p = <0.00001
Removal of child against advice					Chi sq = 3.74
Yes	125	22	33	45	df = 1
No	819	27	38	35	p = 0.053
Other disagreement with social services over plans					Chi sq = 17.91
Yes	182	16	37	47	df = 1
No	762	29	38	33	p = 0.00002

Source: General Questionnaire.

One reason for this may have been the fact that many of the 'events' had taken place at some time in the past. Among those who had started fostering in the past 18 months, experience of an event was strongly associated with intentions to give up.

Minority ethnic carers

Before concluding, we should note some differences between foster carers from minority ethnic groups and the remainder. Minority ethnic foster carers (mainly black and Asian) did not differ from the others in the average length of time for which they had fostered or in the 'average number' of 'events' they experienced. They were, however, significantly less likely to report an event which affected family relationships.

Their mental health as they reported it was also significantly better than that of the majority community, but this seemed to be a reflection of the rather lower number of 'events' they reported – the difference was no longer significant when this number was taken into account. There was no difference between minority ethnic carers and others in the proportion saying that they had ever thought of giving up fostering. There was, however, some slight evidence that 'events' had had a greater effect on the attitude towards fostering among the majority community carers than they had among others, although this interaction was only just significant ($p = 0.04$). Taken as a whole, then, these findings give little ground for thinking that carers from minority ethnic communities are any less in need of support than others.

Conclusions

This chapter has concentrated on the negative 'events' that may be experienced by foster carers. It would be wrong if, as a result, it gave an unbalanced impression of the joys and pains of fostering. Overall, as we have seen, the foster carers were strongly positive about what they were doing. Forty-five per cent strongly agreed, and a further 51 per cent agreed, with the statement that 'We get a lot of satisfaction from fostering'. Only 7 per cent said they definitely intended to give up fostering in the next two years and, where they proposed to do so, this was not necessarily because they were dissatisfied with fostering. Only 18 per cent of carers (fewer than one in five) said that fostering affected their current sense of well-being as we had tried to measure it, albeit they were much more likely than others to have experienced 'events'. These positive findings parallel those of Dando and Minty (1987) who reported that

Type of 'event'	n	Have you ever felt you would like to give up fostering? (%)			Prob. of difference
		Hardly ever/ never	Some-times	Very often/ often	
Breakdown/ disruption					Chi sq = 49.77
Yes	439	38	45	17	df = 1
No	505	61	32	7	p<0.00001
Allegation					Chi sq = 10.92
Yes	149	41	39	20	df = 1
No	795	52	38	10	p = 0.0001
Difficulties with birth parents					Chi sq = 18.23
Yes	229	41	40	19	df = 1
No	715	53	37	10	p = 0.00002
Severe family tensions					Chi sq = 74.07
Yes	290	32	46	23	df = 1
No	654	58	35	7	p<0.00001
Removal of child against advice					Chi sq = 2.25
Yes	125	45	40	15	df = 1
No	819	51	38	11	p = 0.1333
Other disagreement with social services over plans					Chi sq = 8.59
Yes	182	41	42	17	df = 1
No	762	52	37	11	p = 0.0033

Table 6.6 'Events' and an intention of giving up fostering in next two years

Source: General Questionnaire.

three-quarters of their sample of foster carers felt that fostering had had a positive effect on their family.

That much acknowledged, it remains true that fostering is a job which intrudes into family life and which can produce acute distress. The 'events' we have described can simultaneously assault a carer's picture of her- or himself as a caring and effective person, destroy her or his sense of being supported by people they may have seen as colleagues in social services, and produce acute tensions among family members. In some cases, foster carers may feel they have a choice between damaging their own families and failing their foster children. And there are further difficulties that we have not discussed – problems with neighbours or tensions produced by the lengths of time courts take to come to a decision, to name but two. In such circumstances, the provision of effective support becomes a moral imperative, irrespective of any effect it may have on the recruitment, effectiveness and retention of foster carers.

In analysing these issues, this chapter provides support for a number of previous findings. The distressing nature of disruptions has been documented by Aldgate and Hawley (1986) and Berridge and Cleaver (1987). Hicks and Nixon (1989) have already discussed the impact of allegations on foster carers and the way this can be exacerbated by social work practice. Other 'events' have been less commonly discussed, and we hope it is useful to have evidence of their frequency and their apparent impact on mental health and attitude to fostering. (We say 'apparent impact' because causation may not be all one way: strain may lead to less skilful fostering and so to 'events', as well as 'events' leading to strain.) A sizeable minority of foster carers experienced each of these 'events', and a third of those who had been fostering for less than a year had experienced at least one of them. So, too, had two-thirds of the whole sample.

Even so, our analysis will have given a misleadingly low impression of the frequency of the 'events'. Those experiencing these 'events' would probably be more likely to stop fostering. They would thus be less likely to be identified in a study such as ours, which looked at foster carers at a particular point in time and would be less likely to pick up foster carers who gave up quickly.[3] In one respect, our findings seem somewhat at odds with earlier research that describes little reported contact between birth parents and foster carers and little reported trouble either. In this regard, matters may have changed since the Children Act. As we have seen, a quarter of the foster carers reported that they had had difficulties in their relationship with birth families. They also frequently commented on the greater weight given to the views of birth parents or on their involvement in the placement. They could see these factors as contributing to the removal of children against foster carers' own strong advice, placement disruption and, to a lesser extent, disagreements with social services over plans. We cannot comment on the wisdom or otherwise of these decisions.

What is clear from the study is that close involvement with birth parents may expose foster carers to situations in which they feel physically threatened, and where they may believe that the best interests of the child are being sacrificed to what some perceive as dogma. Such a demanding professional role for foster carers carries with it implications for support, remuneration, the provision of information, and care in making practical arrangements (e.g. over where, in certain circumstances, foster children and birth parents should meet).

In conclusion, there is a wide spectrum of difficult experiences that may trouble foster carers. There is a need to look in detail at these 'events', to tease out what bothers the various parties and to consider ways in which good practice might address them. We return to these issues in our concluding chapter.

Notes

1. The chapter itself is reproduced with few changes from an article in the *British Journal of Social Work* (Wilson, Sinclair and Gibbs 2000) and we are grateful to the journal for permission to do this.

2. We tested the relevant associations in two ways, looking first at whether the carer had experienced an event using logistic regression, and then at the mean number of events per event category using multiple regression. Both analyses were consistent in showing that only the age of the oldest first child was significantly associated with our dependent variable, after the number of previous foster children had been taken into account ($p = 0.05$ and $p<0.0001$), a fact which adds weight to the generally held view that older foster children are more difficult than younger ones.

3. It is likely that many people give up fostering after an allegation, even if exonerated. Moreover, the likelihood of responding to the questionnaire was related to the age of the eldest child fostered (the older the child, the less likely the response). As carers fostering older children are more likely to experience 'events', we may have slightly underestimated the number likely to do so. The other respects in which the sample was known to be biased – type of local authority, ethnicity of carer, other paid work, dormant or active carer – were not associated with the number of 'events' experienced, after allowing for time fostering and number of children fostered.

Chapter Seven

Informal and Formal Support

Introduction

We turn now to the effects of informal and formal support. Our interest in this study is primarily in the latter. Informal support is no doubt crucial. From the point of view of social services, however, it is to a large extent given. Social workers cannot create loving spouses or friendly neighbours. They may notice the presence or absence of these supports in selecting foster carers. They may try to compensate for their absence or seek to ensure that the supporters are not overloaded. They may encourage hybrid forms of formal and informal support through, for example, foster carer groups. In the end, however, their power to support foster carers is dependent on their own skills and expertise and on the formal resources such as money and relief breaks that they can access. For these reasons we shall treat informal support briefly.

Informal support

We asked the foster carers to rate each of four possible sources of support – immediate family, other relatives, friends and neighbours – on a simple three-point scale, according to whether they felt they got no support from them, some support or a lot of support. Table 7.1 sets out the resulting distribution.

Despite the crudeness of these measures, Table 7.1 clearly brings out the great importance of families as sources of support, a finding strongly in keeping with those of Farmer and her colleagues (2002). Nearly two-thirds of those replying said that they received a lot of support from this source. The next major source of informal support was friends, with over a third saying that they received a lot of support from them. By contrast, fewer than one in six said that they received much support from neighbours.

Table 7.1 Ratings of sources of informal support				
Source of support	n	None (%)	Some (%)	A lot (%)
Immediate family	925	8	29	63
Other relatives	879	26	50	24
Friends	898	14	51	35
Neighbours	878	45	40	15

Source: General Questionnaire.

The importance of family and, to a lesser extent, other relatives has already been illustrated in the carers' comments quoted in Chapter 4. Rather less was said there about the importance of friends and neighbours. The impression that neighbours and friends were relatively unimportant as sources of support was reinforced by a question in which we asked directly: 'What do you consider the most important support you get?' Neighbours and friends appeared very rarely together and then generally in tandem with others (e.g. 'family and friends'). An exception to this rule was provided by a very small number of carers who clearly got considerable support from a particular friend:

> From my best friend, who just offers help when needed, and also my mother from a distance just telling me I'm doing the best I can.

Where friends were mentioned, their presence as sources of support was sometimes explained as though their help could not naturally be expected:

> As I am a single carer living away from my immediate family I rely a lot on friends and social workers.

As for neighbours, there was evidence that they could often be significant sources of stress. One in five disagreed with the statement 'most of our neighbours think it is a good idea that we foster'. A third agreed with the statement that 'our neighbours are sometimes upset by the behaviour of our foster children'.

Generally the carers said that most people supported what they did ('Most people think it's great what I'm doing'). Nevertheless, a quarter of the sample said that they had experienced criticism or hostility specifically because they fostered. The most common criticism was that the foster carer was 'doing it for the money':

> A lot of people think you only do it for the money. People generally think you are crazy to foster when your own family has grown up and left home.

Other issues were that fostering was considered by others to be unfair on the foster carer's own children, that the foster carer should behave in line with community expectations (e.g. by getting a job) and that the foster children themselves were a bad influence:

> We find if there is any problems at schools or youth groups, our foster children are blamed first. I also find some family members treat foster children differently.

> People avoid you. They react differently with these children and also comment that it's not fair on my own children.

Sometimes these problems stemmed from the behaviour of the foster children themselves:

> When I had a child constantly offending, neighbours got very angry because he used to involve some of their children.

> The girl I have now hit a younger child. About six people not talking to me.

More commonly, however, they were seen as stemming from ignorance or a general lack of sympathy, some with overtones of Victorian days:

> Not right to take them into my home. As you have a lot of responsibility and they are bad children – and the mothers and fathers should look after them themselves instead of parking them off on others to look after them.

> We have been criticised by both family and neighbours. The general feeling seems to be that we are strange people to live with difficult and aggressive children.

Relationship between measures of informal support and outcome
We explored the association between our measures of informal support and three outcome measures: our overall measure of outcome (the 'fostering

score'), our measure of strain ('symptom score') and the strength of the carer's intention to leave over the next two years. The variables we considered were:

1.   Ratings of support from:

   (a) immediate family (1–3)

   (b) other relatives (1–3)

   (c) friends (1–3)

   (d) neighbours (1–3).

2.   Experience of criticism/hostility (1–2).

3.   'Most of our relatives think it a good idea we foster' (1–4).

4.   'Most of our neighbours support what we do as a foster family' (1–4).

5.   'Our neighbours are sometimes upset by the behaviour of our foster children' (1–4).

Almost all these variables were correlated with our measures of outcome in the predicted direction, although many of the associations were not strong.[1]

Relationship between informal support and local authority

Carers rated support from their immediate family more highly in some authorities than others. There were also differences in their readiness to report that their relatives were supportive of their fostering and that their neighbours were not upset by their children's behaviour.[2]

In general the differences in the amount of informal support available to carers in the different authorities were not large.

Formal support

We looked at formal support in five main areas: preparation for fostering, ongoing training, support from social workers, services, and financial support. In each of these areas we will give a brief description of the carers' reactions to the support provided and then try and assess its relationship to our three main measures of outcome: the fostering score, the strain score and intentions to leave. Some of the material on formal support that follows in this and the next chapter is included in an article we published in the journal *Child and Family Social Work* (Fisher *et al.* 2000).

Preparation for fostering

We asked the carers to estimate how many hours of training or preparation they had before starting to foster. Their answers ranged from 'nothing' to 200 with an average of 26. Roughly half the sample had had training of more than 16 hours. While a fifth (21%) had had no training at all, a further fifth had had 40 hours or more, and one in ten said that they had had more than 90 hours. These figures varied between authorities with carers in some authorities reporting much higher hours than those in others. They also varied with the time at which the carer entered fostering. Those who entered more recently tended to report more previous training.

We also asked the carers how far they had felt prepared for their first placement. They gave their answers on a five-point scale ranging from 1 ('very prepared') to 5 ('very unprepared'). Triseliotis and his colleagues (2000) who asked this question found that six out of ten carers were either prepared or well prepared. Our findings were similar. In general, the carers were positive in their answers. Roughly a third (31%) said that they were well prepared and a further third (34%) said that they were prepared. A quarter said 'half and half' and the remainder (one in ten) gave more discouraging answers. Once again there was evidence that more recent recruits felt better prepared than had older ones.[3]

The term 'prepared' was somewhat ambiguous. It could imply that the carers were ready for what they met, perhaps because of previous experiences, or it could mean that they were ready because of the training and other preparation they had received. However the question was interpreted, there was a very highly significant association between the carers' belief that they felt prepared and the amount of training/preparation they reported.

The associations between hours of previous training and other variables were rather less encouraging. The number of hours of preparation was not significantly associated with the number of 'events' experienced or the symptom score. It was (just) significantly associated with the fostering score, but the strength of the association was so low as to be almost negligible. There was, however, a significant association between the number of hours of previous training and an intention not to leave in the next two years.

Closer examination showed that the association between training and the intention to leave was most apparent shortly after the training took place. Among those who had been fostering for two years or less, 80 per cent of those definitely intending to stop had had less than 17 hours' training before starting. The comparable proportion among those who intended to stay was only 40 per cent. By contrast, there was only a slight association between amount of initial training and intentions to leave among those who had been fostering for three years or more.

Given the lack of apparent large effects on variables other than the intention to leave, it seems possible that the main effect of training was as a test of motivation. It was not that training enabled foster carers to handle fostering with less strain, but rather that it gave them a realistic sense of what might be involved. Some might then decide that fostering was not for them. Those who graduated from a relatively substantial period of training or preparation were therefore less dismayed by what they found when they started.

Training after the first placement

Training does not stop with the first placement. We therefore asked the carers to estimate the numbers of hours' training they had received after starting to foster. A quarter volunteered that they had had no training since starting, and a further fifth that they had had no more than ten hours. However, one in six said that they had had between 11 and 20 hours, and a further fifth that they had had 21 to 50 hours. The remainder (about a fifth in all) said that they had had more than this.

Two variables were strongly related to the amount of training after the first placement. First, there was a highly significant variation by local authority ($p<0.0001$). Second, and unsurprisingly, the longer the carer had been fostering, the more training they estimated they had had.

We asked carers whether they had been offered training that they had turned down. Two-thirds said that they had. Table 7.2 gives the proportion of the sample who said they had turned down training for a variety of reasons.

Most of these reasons are self-explanatory. However, 'other' reasons covered a variety of factors, including the illness of the foster carer, the difficulty of leaving a foster child on their own, holidays and other commitments.

Other researchers have found that lone carers (Farmer et al. 2002) or younger carers (Triseliotis et al. 2000) have particular difficulties in attending training. Contrary to what we expected we found that couple carers were rather more likely than others to report a high number of practical difficulties over attending training. We did, however, find that the older the carer the less likely they were to report such practical difficulties, particularly those relating to childcare. Similarly carers who had a foster or other child under five at home were more likely to report difficulties in attending related to childcare. We also found very strong and consistent relationships between the number of difficulties reported and whether the carer worked and – even more strongly – with whether the carer had a working partner. Only a third of those who had a partner at home who was not working reported any practical difficulties as opposed to more than half of those who had one working full-time. The message seems to be that carers in all situations can face practical difficulties in attending and that social services have to take serious account of them in making their practical arrangements.

Table 7.2 Proportions turning down training and reasons given		
Reason for turning down training	*n*	%
Not relevant to needs	212	22
Childcare difficulties	204	21
Clash with work	219	23
Inconvenient time	317	33
Transport difficulties	145	15
Other	96	10
Any reason	627	66
Total	944	

Source: General Questionnaire.
Note: More than one reason could be given, so percentages add to more than 100.

We asked carers if they had had training in a variety of areas and also whether they needed more of it. Some of these areas were clearly age-related. So, for example, nearly a third said that they had neither had, nor needed, training related to delinquency, and a quarter that this was the case in relation to issues about school. Drugs were a further area where both the provision of training and the wish for it were strongly age-related. Most kinds of training were, however, equally desired and provided irrespective of the age of the foster child. Table 7.3 gives the proportions that said they had received some training in the various areas and the proportions that wanted training or further training in that area.

Table 7.3 Proportions with training and wanting further training, by topic area

Possible area of training	n	Received (%)	Want more (%)
Handling disobedience/ difficult behaviour	840	72	51
Drugs	832	57	53
Delinquency	761	43	54
Anxious and depressed	800	49	65
Unaffectionate children	773	45	57
Sexual abuse	853	75	50
Physical abuse	829	75	51
Developmental stages (what to expect at different ages)	786	63	35
Health/first aid	814	60	49
Dealing with birth parents	834	59	42
School issues/education	805	53	40
Issues of sexism/racism	801	64	38
Children Act	824	75	48
Local authority procedures	830	76	53

Source: General Questionnaire.

The numbers responding to the various questions were often substantially below the total in the sample (944). The numbers answering tended to be low when a high proportion of those who did answer said they had not received any training in that area. So the overall impression, that most areas were covered by most of the sample, probably needs to be qualified. Many of those who had not received any training in the area may not have answered the question. In some cases, training may not have been relevant. For example, the lowest number of respondents was found in relation to delinquency, which would not be relevant for those caring for very young children.

Overall, we found that eight out of ten foster carers wanted some or further training in at least one of the areas we listed. The areas of highest demand involved courses that dealt with anxious or depressed children and (among carers of teenagers) for courses that dealt with delinquency.

We also asked the foster carers to rate their satisfaction with various aspects of training – specifically its amount, relevance and quality. In each case, around 60 per cent expressed themselves satisfied with the training, with a further quarter to a third expressing themselves very satisfied. Generally, their written comments expressed gratitude for specialist subjects which 'ordinary' parents might not be expected to have at their finger tips (notably on drugs and sexual abuse). There was also appreciation for training carried out by other foster carers and for the chance to meet other carers. This was sometimes accompanied by a feeling that foster carer expertise was insufficiently valued, that particular topics were taught which were of little relevance to the carer's situation, or that too little account was taken of the difficulties of attending training, particularly those associated with work and with leaving foster children. Triseliotis and his colleagues (2000) similarly report the value which carers place on involving other carers in training.

Satisfaction with training in any respect rose with the number of hours of training reported. It was also significantly associated with all our three outcome measures.[4] The associations may represent an impact of high quality training on stress and outcomes. However, the very weak or absent relationship between number of hours' training and our three measures argues against a causal impact of training. The effect could also run the other way. Unstressed carers who intended to stay in fostering could be more appreciative of training. Certainly, authorities that provided more training did not appear to have keener or less stressed carers.

Overall, therefore, training seemed to have achieved quite a wide coverage of topics. Foster carers, who valued specialist input and the opportunity to learn from other carers, generally welcomed it. There were, however, a number of practical difficulties that sometimes made it hard for carers to make use of the training on offer. The training was rarely intensive – less than a fifth of the carers had had more than 50 hours of it. Also, although some authorities appeared to have invested more in it than others, there was no evidence that this difference in investment was reflected in differences in the outcome measures we have used.

Meeting with other carers

As foster carers appreciate learning from each other, it would seem logical to provide them with opportunities to meet. We asked the carers whether their authority ran regular groups for foster carers in their area so that they could talk about fostering. Eighty-five per cent said that the authority did. Almost all those who said otherwise came from three authorities where between a quarter and a sixth of carers said that there were no such groups in their particular area.

We also asked the carers how often they attended these groups and whether they had contact with individual foster carers from whom they could ask advice or get practical help. Finally, we asked them to rate how much practical and emotional support they received from other carers using a simple three-point scale that ran from 1 ('none') to 3 ('a lot').

Overall, a third of those able to attend fostering groups said they did so regularly, and nearly a third that they never attended at all. (Regular attendance was least likely among the better educated carers and among those who had work – findings which suggest that social mix and the need for company out of home played a part in encouraging use of groups. Couple carers and carers with working partners were no more or less likely to attend.) Most, nearly 70 per cent, said that they could turn to another foster carer for practical help and advice. A quarter said that they received a lot of support from other foster carers while a third said that they received none.

Unsurprisingly, these different markers of support from foster carers were strongly related. Nearly three-quarters (73%) of those reporting that there were foster carer groups in their area said that they were able to call on another carer for help and advice. The comparable figure for those reporting no such groups was only 51 per cent. Similarly, 70 per cent of those who reported groups in their area said that they gained at least some support from other carers. The comparable proportion for those without the opportunity to attend groups was 50 per cent.

Those who attended the groups regularly were particularly likely to feel that they could call on another foster carer – nine out of ten said that they could do so. Again, only half of those who had the opportunity to attend groups but never did so reported the availability of support from other carers.

There was some evidence that the availability of groups, attendance at groups, being able to turn to other carers and perceived support from other foster carers were related to our outcome measures.[5]

So it seems that foster care groups play a valued role in introducing foster carers to each other. They may also play a part in reducing the strain on carers or in enhancing their commitment to foster care. They are not, however, available in all areas or equally appreciated by all carers. In these respects our findings are in line with the great majority of British research in this area (see, for example, Farmer *et al.* 2002; Thoburn, Norford and Rashid 2000; Triseliotis *et al.* 2000; Walker *et al.* 2002).

Support from family placement workers and other social workers

Social workers provide a potentially important source of direct support for foster carers. They are also a gateway to other kinds of support, such as relief breaks. The great majority of foster carers in the study had access to two kinds of social worker – a link worker or family placement worker who was, as it were, the family's social worker, and the child's social worker who dealt with the individual child. Overall, 95 per cent of the sample said that they had 'a social worker who supports you other than social worker for the individual child'. Nearly half of those who did not came from one particular authority.

Asked to rate the amount of support they received from these sources, the carers were decidedly more favourable to the family placement workers. Fifty-five per cent said that they received a lot of support from this worker. By contrast, only 36 per cent said that they had a lot of support from the child's social worker. At the other end of the scale, 10 per cent said that they received no support from the child's social worker and 6 per cent that they received none from the family placement worker. (Half of the latter reported that they did not have such a worker.)

The carers' requirements of these social workers were simple and understandable. They should respect the carer, visit promptly when asked, be efficient and expeditious in sorting out difficulties with the local authority, listen to both child and carer, work as a team with the carer, do what they promise and provide good advice. In the view of the carers, a number of social workers failed these tests:

I find the way she seems to talk down to me very unhelpful to me personally.

Raises hopes on sibling contact and then is not able to achieve what he promises.

A little slow in sorting out financial problems – the dreaded paper work. Only seems to come in a crisis. Often has not done things that are requested. Does not seem to have enough time to go round.

Seems to be on leave so often that requests for assistance often have to wait for well over a week from initial contact. Never communicates the child's feelings after having interviews with her (a little feedback would be useful).

As implied by the ratings given earlier, these negative comments mainly applied to the child's social worker and even there were outweighed by positive ones. These positive comments were largely the mirror image of the negative ones:

Agrees with our strategies and supports as necessary, endeavours to involve other professionals as appropriate, supports in difficult school situations, is approachable and human.

Turns up, talks and sorts! Previous social worker never appeared at all so this is a novelty for us. Current social worker is more than helpful, understands the child and is always there to help.

Is there when we need advice, helped us to get mainstream placement at day nursery when we were told no. Transport at short notice for appointments or day nursery when my car breaks down. Sorts out back pay for disability living allowance.

A particular strength of social workers could be their long knowledge of the child:

She knows Michael and understands him and his past. This helps him as she has been with him in good times and bad times with his father and mother.

Running through the comments was the common theme that the social worker should be 'there for you'. Social workers who were seen as failing to return telephone calls, as frequently ill, as always in meetings, or as often on holiday or on courses, were not appreciated. Understandably social workers in pressurised area offices were more likely than family placement workers to be the subjects of these complaints. This fact, along with differences in role, no doubt partly explains the well-validated result that children's social workers are less appreciated than link workers and that difficulties in contacting social workers and their lack of reliability are key complaints (see, particularly, Farmer *et al.* 2002 and Triseliotis *et al.* 2000).

We assessed the amount of support from social workers and family placement workers through the support ratings described above. We also asked a series of more specific questions about the family placement workers. These focused on the workers' reliability, ability to listen, availability, appreciativeness, responsiveness and ability to provide good advice. The questions yielded a highly reliable measure (alpha = 0.93) of 'family placement worker supportiveness'.

Family placement workers who were often in contact were seen as more supportive. Eighty-three per cent of the carers who said their family placement worker visited as often as two weekly or more said they provided 'a lot of support'. Only a third of the carers reporting monthly or more infrequent visits were equally appreciative. Unfortunately, fortnightly visits were the exception. Only 14 per cent of carers reported them, while 44 per cent were visited less often than monthly. Frequent telephone contact was also associated with assessments of social worker supportiveness (perhaps because foster carers were more likely to telephone workers they perceived as supportive).

The perceived supportiveness of the family placement worker and the child's social worker were significantly associated with our all three of our measures of outcome. The correlations were not large (from a statistical point of view they never accounted for more than 4% of the variation). Their impact on perceived support was much greater.[6]

Social workers and link workers are therefore highly important elements in the foster carers' system of support. However, commitment to fostering, decisions to leave fostering and the carer's mental health are subject to a wide range of influences over and above the formal support the carer receives. In relation to these broader outcomes, social workers play a much smaller, although arguably significant, part.

Other sources of support

We asked the carers about the supportiveness, or otherwise, of a variety of local authority arrangements (see Table 7.4). At first sight, the replies suggested a reasonable degree of satisfaction. Carers expressed most dissatisfaction with the information they received about former foster children (47%) and the out-of-hours service (38%). They appeared relatively satisfied with the arrangements for handling abuse and with their involvement in plans for their foster child.

Table 7.4 Carers' satisfaction with local authority arrangements					
Arrangement for	n	Very satisfied (%)	Satisfied (%)	Dis-satisfied (%)	Very dis-satisfied (%)
Allegations	621	22	57	13	8
Involving you in plans for foster child	864	25	57	15	3
Breaks for you	788	18	51	22	9
Telling you what happens to children who have left	806	13	40	30	17
Response out of hours / at weekends	805	14	48	26	12

Source: General Questionnaire.

In some cases, however, this satisfaction may have arisen from ignorance. This seems to have been so in the case of allegations. Many of those who replied to the questionnaire did not answer the question about allegations, presumably because they felt they did not have the experience to do so. Among those who had not experienced an allegation, 16 per cent were dissatisfied or very dissatisfied with the arrangements. The comparable figure for those who had experienced one was 40 per cent.

In a rather similar way, dissatisfaction with the out-of-hours service climbs steadily with the age of the foster children. We divided the carers into four roughly equal groups, in terms of the average age of their foster children. The proportion of carers who were dissatisfied grew from 25 per cent in the group with the youngest children to 33 per cent in the next, 40 per cent in the next and 47 per cent among the highest age group. Comments suggested that the out-of-hours service was commonly criticised for knowing little about foster care and likely to put off dealing with problems rather than resolving them – complaints that echo those made to other researchers (Farmer *et al.* 2002; Triseliotis *et al.* 2000). The steady growth in dissatisfaction with the age of foster child may reflect the fact that those with most need of the service, or most experience of it, were the most critical.

Carers in different authorities appraised the out-of-hours service differently. Three-quarters of the carers in one authority expressed satisfaction with the out-of-hours service as against just over four out of ten in another. It seems likely that this, and a comparable difference in relation to satisfaction with breaks (where the satisfied varied from 41% to 74%), reflects real differences in the quality of these aspects of support for carers in the different areas. The differences do not seem simply to mirror differences in general attitudes towards the authority. If this were so, one would expect the same authorities to score 'best' in relation to each area of service. This was not the case.

Financial support

As we saw in Chapter 4, the arguments advanced by foster carers for greater financial support were based on three main strands. First, lack of finance was seen as hindering the quality of foster care itself – for example, the foster carer's ability to provide extras for the foster children. Second, it was argued that foster care was not equivalent to 'ordinary parenting'. It was a stressful job involving such things as attendance at courts, and one which had particular disadvantages – lack of pension entitlement, insecure funding dependent on the availability of foster children, and particular expenses connected with wear and tear on the house, transport and so on. Equity demanded a higher fee. Third, it was felt that an increase in pay or allowances would make it easier to recruit foster carers.

The basic thrust of these arguments was that allowances and or pay should be increased. However, there were related concerns. In particular, some foster carers felt that the basis of payment was inequitable (e.g. that allowances should be higher for babies) and others that the arrangements for payment were inefficient (e.g. that it was very difficult to get money back which had been spent on transport, or to learn about entitlements).

Evidence on the actual level of payments was collected through two questions. Of these, one asked: 'How much are you receiving per week in foster care allowances/enhanced allowances/fees?' A second asked: 'Over the last three months, roughly how much have you had in "one-off payments", e.g. help with holidays?'

In analysing these replies, we first considered only those who were currently fostering at least one child. Their average income from fees and allowances was £162 per week, after excluding those who were getting nothing.

There was, however, considerable variation. One third said that they were getting no more than £87 per week. A further third were getting between £88 and £168. A final third were getting in excess of this, a small minority very much more than this, to a maximum for a carer with three foster children of £2100 per week.

The answers on 'one-off payments' suggested that just over four in ten (43% of those currently fostering) had received no such payments in the past. The average payment over the three months was £133. This suggests that, on average, one-off payments constitute a relatively small proportion of the average income from fostering – around £10 out of £162. Nevertheless, there was very considerable variation and for some the sums were large. Two-thirds had received either nothing or no more than £130. Ninety per cent received £300 or less. However, one individual recorded £6000 and another £3000.

The average amounts received by a foster family were strongly influenced by the local authority with whom they were registered and the number of children they fostered (see Table 7.5).

Table 7.5 Average weekly income (£) from fostering by local authority and number of foster children

Authority	Number of children						Overall average
	0	1	2	3	4	5	
Area 1	70	147	297	613	348	–	265
Area 2	47	79	124	212	237	180	104
Area 3	83	174	252	385	423	267	218
Area 4	93	92	137	228	333	362	143
Area 5	77	100	127	198	197	300	126
Area 6	162	171	201	319	590	–	228
Area 7	56	100	166	235	191	188	131

Source: General Questionnaire.

As can be seen, many of those with no foster children still claimed to be receiving some weekly allowance from their local authority, probably, although we did not ask, in the form of a 'retainer' fee. In most authorities this was about half the amount paid when they had one child but in local Areas 4 and 6, it was roughly equivalent to the allowance for one child. However, the most notable feature of Table 7.5 lies in the large differences between authorities in the average amounts paid out. This was highest in the two London authorities and the Home Counties authority, where the average was over twice that recorded in Area 2.

Three other variables were strongly related to weekly income from fostering – whether or not the carer worked (other things being equal, working carers were paid less), the average age of the foster children and the type of fostering undertaken (project foster carers, for example, received more than others). We used these variables to predict the level of income the foster carers could expect.[7]

We had expected our analysis to account for more of the variation in income than it did. One reason for our failure to explain more of the variance was that we had no direct measure of the difficulty of the children and young people involved. Difficult behaviour was clearly one criterion for paying foster carers more in the authorities (a fact which was illustrated in part by complaints from individual foster carers that they had not been compensated for the strains imposed on them by a particularly difficult child). However, it is likely that chance – the presence, for example, of a family placement worker who persuasively argues the carer's case – also plays a part. One of the purposes of predicting the level of income was to see whether those foster carers who were 'doing better' financially than might have been expected had different subjective views of the level of payment or allowances they received.

As reported earlier, we gathered statistical evidence on carers' views of their remuneration through a series of six statements set out in Table 7.6. The figures given do not provide a ringing endorsement of the financial rewards for foster carers. Only a minority of foster carers agreed that the payments they received were generous. A slight majority thought that the basis of payment was unfair. Quite substantial minorities thought that their authorities did not let them know about their entitlements and were neither quick nor efficient about paying.

These questions highlighted substantial and highly significant differences between authorities. Depending on the authority, the proportions that agreed or agreed strongly that the authority paid generously varied from 23 per cent to 46 per cent. Agreement that the authority was quick and efficient over paying varied from a low of 30 per cent to a high of 62 per cent. There were similar variations in relation to knowledge of entitlements (45% to 71%) and the fairness of payment (38% to 61%).

Table 7.6 Views on aspects of pay and allowances

Aspects of pay and allowances	n	Strongly agree (%)	Agree (%)	Disagree (%)	Strongly disagree (%)
The authority's payment to foster carers is generous	906	5	26	43	26
The basis on which the authority pays foster carers is fair	903	4	43	36	17
Foster care is a job of work and should be salaried appropriately	911	40	34	20	6
Without the fees from fostering we would not continue fostering	909	24	38	26	12
The authority lets us know what we are entitled to	924	10	51	25	14
The authority is quick and efficient over paying	923	12	45	27	16

Source: General Questionnaire.

The most obvious explanation for the differences is that they reflect variations in the efficiency of the authorities and in the level of their payments to foster carers. It was indeed true that the authorities which made higher levels of payments than would be expected on the basis of the age of foster children, type of fostering, and so on, tended to be perceived as more generous. One authority, for example, paid less than others and had the lowest proportion of foster carers perceiving it as generous. Nor was there any apparent reason for the very low proportion of foster carers seeing another authority as quick and efficient over paying other than the obvious one – to wit that it was less efficient than the others.

As a check on these assumptions, we looked at the relationship between the size of income from foster care and perceptions of the authority as generous and the payments as fair. There was a significant correlation between perceptions of generosity (but not fairness) and the size of income from fostering. Carers were also more likely to see the authority as generous if they were receiving more than would have been predicted from information about the age and number of foster children and the type of fostering undertaken. Such carers were also more likely to see the authority as fair.

How far did the size of income and the perceptions of this affect our outcome measures? Carers who were getting more income than predicted were slightly more likely to have higher strain scores. These carers probably took more difficult children. They were also slightly less likely to plan to stop fostering. They did not differ from other carers in our 'attitude to fostering' score.

Conclusions

The results we have given are limited in two ways. We have not explained a high proportion of the variation in the outcome variables of interest. In so far as we have explained the variation, we have not proved beyond all reasonable doubt that the associations have to do with cause and effect.

So much acknowledged, the findings are in keeping with common sense and the correlations, depressed by measurement error, are likely to reflect larger underlying associations. We cannot prove that the correlations reflect cause and effect. It is probably sensible to proceed on the assumption that many of them do.

Briefly, our findings have emphasised:

- *The importance of informal support*

   Whereas it may not be possible for social workers to influence the level of this support, it is a variable that might be assessed in selecting foster carers. Support from families and relatives seems particularly crucial, although neighbours can have a negative effect.

- *The value and limitations of training*

   Training is rarely intensive, and variations between authorities in the amount of training available were not reflected in variations in our outcome measures. At the same time training is valued by foster carers as offering a chance to meet other foster carers, and to learn about issues which ordinary parents may not encounter. There was some criticism that insufficient account was taken of the differing needs of foster carers for training, the difficulty of getting to training associated with work and the need to provide childcare. Conversely there was praise for training that relied on experienced foster carers.

- *The value of foster carer groups*

  These were not universally available and, where they were not, only a minority made very regular use of them. They were, however, valued for themselves and they seemed to facilitate links between individual foster carers that could provide support.

- *The value of social work support*

  Foster carers appreciated social workers who visited regularly, respected the foster carers' work, listened carefully, gave informed advice and responded reliably to requests. Family placement social workers were highly valued with their perceived value increasing with the frequency of their visits. Social workers who were perceived as frequently sick, on holiday, on courses or in meetings and who did not return calls were not appreciated.

- *The impact of foster care allowances*

  There were very large differences between authorities in the level of allowances. Relatively high levels seemed to have some impact on the willingness of foster carers to continue fostering, but did not have an impact on the fostering score or the measure of strain. Income may therefore be an important part of any strategy designed to ensure foster carer retention, but needs to be accompanied by other measures designed to reduce strain. Considerable irritation is caused to foster carers by failures to keep them adequately informed of their entitlements and to ensure that the financial aspects of fostering are handled quickly and efficiently. This was an area where one authority in particular seemed to have considerable scope for improvement.

- *The value of other supportive provisions*

  There was evidence that breaks and out-of-hours service were important in increasing satisfaction with fostering and reducing strain. Out-of-hours service seemed to be particularly important where predicted income (and hence probably difficulty of foster children) was relatively high.

Recently Farmer and her colleagues (2002) have put forward the idea that foster carers need a 'net of support' and that this is only as strong as its weakest link. Triseliotis and his colleagues (2000) have similarly emphasised the need for all aspects of support for carers to be of a high standard. Our findings certainly support these particular conclusions, and reinforce other findings on what carers like and do not like about social work and other forms of intended support. Foster carers need to be supported financially, through training and contacts with other carers, through good out-of-hours services, short breaks if required, and support from the child's and their own social worker. A good service should, in our view, have all these things in place.

Notes

1.   Out of 24 correlations between the variables and our outcome measures, only three failed to reach significance at the 0.05 level. Support from friends was not significantly associated with the strain score or with intentions to leave ($p = 0.097$). Support from neighbours was not related to intentions to leave. However, although most of the correlations were significant at the 0.001 level or beyond, this reflected the size of the sample rather than the strength of the correlations which, when significant, varied between 0.093 (still significant in a sample of this size, although it accounts for a negligible amount of the variation) and the rather more impressive 0.43 (between the belief that relatives support fostering and the fostering score).

2.   These three differences were significant on a one-way analysis of variance ($p.05$) but only the differences on the ratings of support from friends were highly significant ($p = 0.002$).

3.   Here there was less evidence of variation between authorities, although a test using a one-way analysis of variance verged on significance ($p = 0.07$).

4.   The actual correlations, however, were very highly significant but quite small (they varied from 0.16 to 0.32).

5.   Most of the predicted relationships were significant and in the predicted direction, and some of the associations were very highly significant. Nevertheless, the correlations were all small, and none accounted for more than 2 per cent of the variation.

6.   Taken together, our measure of support from the child's social worker and our link worker acceptability score accounted for 25 per cent of the variation in the carer's rating of satisfaction with 'the support you get as a foster family'.

7.   More specifically, we used a stepwise multiple regression with each local authority and type of foster care entered as a dummy variable. The analysis accounted for around a third of the variation (the exact figure depending on whether we transformed the dependent variable so that it was less skewed).

Chapter Eight

Continuing and Ceasing to Foster

Introduction

Current policy aims to increase the number of carers and so enable a greater choice of placements. One way of achieving this is more effective recruitment. Another is to reduce the turnover among carers. The hope is that better support will achieve this second goal.

Against this background, the present chapter compares foster carers who cease fostering with those who continue. It examines:

- what proportion of carers cease to foster

- what factors, including support, seem to predict this behaviour.

Method

As already discussed, in September 1997, we asked family placement social workers in our authorities to give us brief information on all the carers registered in their authorities. This yielded some information on 1416 foster carers out of a possible total of 1528, a response rate of over 93 per cent. We repeated this exercise approximately 19 months later, in April 1999, and obtained data on 1477 carers who had been eligible for the original survey – a response rate of 97 per cent.

On both occasions the non-responses were clustered in particular geographical areas. In the first census, these areas were localised within authorities. On the second occasion, most non-responses came from a particular local authority that had installed a computer system and was experiencing difficulties in retrieving information. Such difficulties meant that the period of follow-up varied from 15 to 23 months, with an average of around 18 or 19. The census covered all those to whom we sent the General Questionnaire, so we could also use information from this questionnaire to compare those who stayed and who continued.

Rates of ceasing to foster

Triseliotis and his colleagues (2000) reported an annual loss of around 8 or 9 per cent among 1184 'active carers' in Scotland, although they considered that this was perhaps an underestimate of 1 or 2 per cent. They also quoted an NFCA survey (Waterhouse 1997) that reported that three-quarters of English authorities who were able to give figures quoted percentages just under 10 per cent.

These figures assume a definition of 'ceasing to foster' and of the base used to calculate turnover. In our study, these definitions were more problem-atic than expected. Table 8.1 compares the outcomes for carers who were con-sidered active at the first census with outcomes for 'inactive' carers who were still registered. The four outcomes are 'actively fostering' (which includes a small number waiting for an identified foster child), 'vacancy' (which covers those who were expected to continue fostering but had no current child), 'in-active' (which covers those not expected to foster again) and 'not registered'.

Table 8.1 Proportions ceasing to foster among active and inactive carers

	Status at Census 2				
Status at Census 1	Active	Vacancy	Inactive	No reg.	Total
Active and vacancy	900 (77%)	53 (4%)	89 (8%)	130 (11%)	1172
Inactive	30 (27%)	14 (13%)	26 (23%)	41 (37%)	111
Total	930 (73%)	67 (5%)	115 (9%)	171 (13%)	1283

Sources: Census 1 and Census 2.

Among the 1283 carers for whom we had the relevant information at both points in time, nearly three-quarters (73%) were said to be currently fostering. A further 5 per cent were said to be waiting to be allocated a new foster child. This leaves a total of 23 per cent who were either said to be inactive or to be no longer registered. Rather more than half of these (13%) were said to be no longer registered.

One definition of turnover would be the annual proportion of registered carers who were no longer registered at the end of the year. Given the fact that our follow-ups probably average around 18 to 19 months, this would give an annual estimate of around 8 to 9 per cent. This is close to the figures given by Triseliotis et al. (2000) and to the estimate we gave based on figures from the General Questionnaire.

The difficulty with an approach to measuring rates that relies on registration is that authorities seem to differ in the zeal with which they deregister carers. The proportion of carers who were judged inactive/not registered was very similar between authorities. However, the proportion of these who were deregistered varied from 14 per cent to 83 per cent.

A second approach would be to calculate the proportion of carers who had been deemed 'active' who became inactive or were no longer registered. This approach yields a rate of loss of around 19 per cent, and an annual loss of around 12 per cent – somewhat higher than Triseliotis et al.'s (2000) figure.

It could be argued that this approach is somewhat pessimistic. Forty per cent of those who were deemed inactive at the time of the first census were said to be either fostering (27%) or ready to do so (13%). If one estimates that 40 per cent of those said to be inactive at the second census would also reappear as foster carers, this would be a true loss of around 16 per cent of active carers and an annual estimate of around 10 per cent.

The important point is that Triseliotis and his colleagues' (2000) figure is likely to be as relevant to England as to Scotland. The proportions leaving fostering are now far lower than those suggested by Jones' study in 1975. On the Scottish figures, and ours, they are somewhere around 10 per cent in large agencies. What the exact proportion is depends on how the rate is calculated. If comparisons are to be made between authorities, common definitions shall have to be adopted. For most practical purposes, a figure of around 10 per cent is probably good enough.

Who leaves and who stays?

We turn next to the question of who leaves and who stays. We define 'stayers' as those who are currently fostering or who are expected to do so in the future. 'Leavers' are those who are either no longer fostering or who are not expected to do so again. As discussed above, some 'leavers' will in fact foster again. However, any separation of stayers and leavers is rough and ready. The one we have made has the advantage of not being unduly influenced by local author- ity practice (all authorities have similar proportions of stayers and leavers).

In this chapter, we compare the leavers and stayers on one variable at a time, using the census where possible and otherwise the General Question- naire. In our next chapter, we try to develop a more complex 'multi-variate' explanation.

Ethnicity, sex and age

The proportions staying and leaving did not differ by ethnicity (although Asian carers were somewhat more likely to leave than others). The small number of male carers was nearly twice as likely to leave as female carers but the difference was not statistically significant.

There was some evidence that age was related to leaving. Thirty-three per cent of carers under 35 left over the follow-up period. They were twice as likely to do so as the main body of carers aged between 35 and 55 (the age group into which three-quarters of carers fall). Carers over 55 were also more likely to cease caring (27% did so – Chi square = 17.73, df = 2, p = 0.001.)

The older age group may be those who see themselves as 'retiring' or who are committed to a particular child who leaves the care system and do not want to take another. There is more uncertainty over the increased turnover among those under 35, which was not noted in Triseliotis *et al.*'s (2000) study or anticipated by what foster carers wrote to us. Possibly they may find foster- ing fits in less well with their lives, react more negatively to strain or an 'event' than anticipated, or they may review their commitment to fostering when their younger children enter school.

Educational level

Triseliotis and his colleagues (2000) found that, at least among women, those who have larger houses and non-manual occupations were more common among their sample of former than current carers.

Our measures of these variables were less good than theirs. However, we did find that better educated (and hence probably better-off) carers were more common among 'inactive' carers at the time of the first census.

However, educational level, as estimated by the social workers, was not related to leaving. Nor did we find that families where everyone always had a bedroom to themselves were more or less likely to continue with fostering.

Work status

The greater preponderance of better-educated carers among the inactive was explained by the fact that more of them were working. As already discussed, it was work that seemed to be the primary factor distinguishing the active from the 'inactive'.

As with education, however, we found no evidence that involvement in work predicted leaving fostering. There seems to be a contradiction between this finding and the fact that working carers were more likely to be 'inactive'. A possible explanation is that work does not produce a move from foster care but may be part of the transition from it. Thus, carers may leave to get a job, rather than leave because they have one.

Family composition: couples and lone carers

Triseliotis and his colleagues (2000) found that lone carers were somewhat more likely than others to cease fostering. The difference, however, was small and non-significant. Our own findings were similar, although in our case the difference was almost significant (26% v. 20% – Chi square = 3.46, df = 1, $p = 0.0627$).

We saw earlier that lone carers did not find fostering more stressful than others. They may, however, be more vulnerable to emergencies – for example, their own illness. If this were so, one would expect that informal support would be particularly important to them. There was some evidence that this was so – the association between leaving and being a lone carer was particularly strong for those who said they did not receive a lot of support from their family (34% v. 20%). By contrast, there was virtually no difference between the leaving rates of couples and lone carers when they reported that they received a lot of support from their families (20% v. 19%).[1] Farmer and her colleagues (2002) have recently reported rather similar findings, suggesting that lone carers fostering adolescents have lower levels of support than others and that friends are particularly important to them.

A question about support from other relatives produced a similar contrast. The leaving rates when support was said to be high was lower among the lone carers (15% v. 22%). By contrast, it was higher when support was said to be 'some or none' (27% as against 20%).

The data consistently suggest that informal support from close family and relatives is important in enabling lone carers to continue fostering. It is less important and may not even be important at all for couples.

Family composition: presence of children

We found no difference between the 'leavers' and 'stayers' in terms of the average number of children they had had, the number of children in their house or the average age of the children in their house. In these respects, our findings differ from those of Triseliotis and his colleagues (2000), who found that former carers had a rather larger number of dependent children. There seems no obvious explanation for this difference.

Fostering experience and numbers of current foster children

There was no association between continuing and the number of children a carer had taken. The number of years for which the carer had fostered was similarly unrelated to leaving or staying.

The larger the number of children the carer currently fostered, the more likely she was to continue. In part, this association arose because those who were not fostering any child included those seen as 'inactive'. However, even if this group were omitted, the relationship continued to be very highly significant (see Table 8.2).

Table 8.2 Number of children fostered at first census by whether carer continued						
		Number of children				
Status	*n*	0	1	2	3	4
Continue	988	57	75	87	93	98
Leave	283	43	25	13	7	2
Total	1271	18	40	26	12	4

Sources: Census 1 and General Questionnaire.
Chi square = 106.48, df = 4, $p<0.00001$. Chi square = 40.59, df = 3, $p<0.00001$ (omitting those with no foster children).

The most likely explanation for this finding concerns the nature of the foster carer's commitment. If a carer is committed to a particular child, she may define herself as parenting an individual rather than providing a service, so she may cease fostering when one child leaves. Carers fostering more than one child are less likely to be in this position. The departure of one child does not 'clear the decks'. They continue to have obligations to others.

It is also likely that carers committed to fostering in general may be more likely to take more children than those who see fostering as a sort of 'adoption'. In these circumstances, fostering is more likely to be part of the carer's way of life. The income from it may be necessary even if not generous, and the enterprise may be more central to the way a carer defines her occupation. For these reasons, a carer taking more than one child may be more likely to continue than one taking only one.

Relative ages of foster children and carers' children

We found no evidence that the average difference in age between carers' children and the foster children was related to leaving. We did, however, find that the average age of foster children among leavers was greater than their average age among those who stayed (11.3 as against 9.5, $p = 0.012$).

One reason for this could be the turnover among foster carers of older foster children who were particularly committed to them, and who ceased fostering with their foster child. In keeping with this suggestion, we found that the loss among foster carers looking after one foster child who was aged 15 or more at the time of the General Questionnaire was particularly high. Indeed, it was three times greater than the loss in the rest of the population (a highly significant difference, $p = 0.0012$).

A second possible reason for the higher average age of the foster children could be that older children are more difficult. If so, one would expect the difference to remain after the omission of children over 15 in single placements (the group referred to earlier). We did this and the difference disappeared. In other words the possibly greater difficulty of older children does not seem to be a reason for the greater turnover of their carers. The loss of carers following the departure of older children whom they were 'seeing through' remains the most likely explanation.

Fostering experience: type of fostering

We were interested in any relationship between the type of fostering and turnover. Our hypothesis was that the more precise the role the foster carers were given, the greater their satisfaction would be, and hence the less their turnover. As can be seen from Table 8.3, we were mistaken.

The highest turnover is among the group of carers whom we coded as having 'other' registrations. This is an artefact of the coding as it included a high proportion of carers whom the social workers considered 'inactive'. The next highest group were relative carers – presumably they stop caring when

Table 8.3 Type of fostering and proportion ceasing fostering		
Type of fostering	*n*	Cease (%)
Long-term	324	26
Relative	89	34
Task	122	26
Relief	115	30
Short	336	23
Long and other	104	16
Task and other	102	25
Short and other	105	10
Other	83	57
Total	1380	26

Sources: Census 1 and Census 2.
Chi square = 68.22, df = 8, $p<0.00001$.

the placement finishes. The lowest turnover was found among those groups that included at least two categories of registration (e.g. short and other). Having a single registration category is therefore associated with a higher turnover, not the reverse.

As we made clear above, this finding was not predicted. Its interpretation must be a matter for speculation. One possibility is that the association reflects the relative flexibility or otherwise of the carers. On this interpretation, those who were prepared to take on a range of fostering roles would be most likely to be registered as suitable for more than one. They might therefore be less likely to cease fostering on the grounds that they were getting work for which they were not prepared.

A second possibility is that it simply reflects the effect of the number of foster children in the household. There was a strong relationship between the number of roles for which approved and the number of children taken. The proportion approved for more than one role rose steadily from 28 per cent where the carer took only one child, to 60 per cent where the carer was fostering five (Chi square for trend = 28.82, df = 1, $p.0001$). The reason may be that dual recognition represents in some sense a response to a situation rather than a preparation for it. Carers are registered for another role when they are asked to diverge from their own.[2]

In practice, however, the association between the number of roles and the number of children did not explain why those with more roles were less likely to leave. When we used both, in an attempt to predict which carers continued, the number of roles remained significant.

Support

Informal support

As we have seen there is evidence that informal support from relatives and family is important in enabling lone carers to continue fostering. We found no evidence that lone carers were particularly likely to continue fostering if supported by neighbours and friends. Nor could we find evidence that any form of informal support enabled couples to continue fostering.

Much to our surprise, carers who said that neighbours were sometimes upset by the behaviour of their foster children were significantly less likely to cease fostering ($p = 0.02$). This may be a chance finding. Alternatively, the fact that they had survived these stresses is perhaps an indicator of their commitment. Carers who reported such hostility were significantly more likely to say that they got a lot of satisfaction from fostering and that fostering enriched their lives.

Training

Contrary to our earlier findings on intention to leave, there was no evidence that the number of hours' training prior to fostering was related to continuance, either among those who had started caring in the last two years, or among all carers. The carer's feeling that she was unprepared or well-prepared for her first placement was similarly unrelated to whether or not she continued.

We did find that the more hours' training the carer reported, the less likely she was to cease fostering. This association was barely significant ($p = 0.04$), and may reflect the greater commitment of those who attend training, rather than the impact of training itself. There is no association between the carer's satisfaction with the quantity, quality and relevance of training and whether or not she continued.

Attendance at fostering groups

Those who had fostering groups in their area were less likely to cease fostering than those who did not. The difference, however, was only 5 per cent and not significant. If fostering groups were available, those who attended regularly were more likely to continue than those who attended occasionally. These, in turn, were more likely to continue than those who never attended. Again, the difference was not significant.

Those who never attended, either from choice or because no groups were available, were significantly less likely to continue. As was the case with training, the differences involved were small, and the interpretation ambiguous. We think it most likely that attendance at these groups both reflects and enhances commitment to foster care.

Having a particular foster carer with whom to discuss practical matters or get advice was also associated with continuing. Again, however, the difference was not significant.

More predictive was a simple rating made by the carer of the extent of the support she received from other carers. As can be seen from Table 8.4, those who perceived themselves as receiving little support from other carers were more likely to cease fostering.

Table 8.4 Support from other carers and ceasing to foster		
Rating of support	n	Cease (%)
None	258	28
Some	336	18
A lot	198	16
Total	792	20

Sources: General Questionnaire, Census 1 and Census 2.
Mantel-Haenszel test for trend, Chi square = 10.56, df = 1, p = 0.0012.
Chi square = 12.50, df = 2, p = 0.0019.

Family placement social worker visits and support

Almost all those responding to the General Questionnaire said that they had a family placement social worker. The minority who did not were less likely to continue fostering. Thirty-two per cent ceased doing so, as opposed to 20 per cent of the remainder. This difference, however, was not statistically significant (Chi square = 3.11, df = 1, p = 0.0776).

There was a similar, but non-significant, trend in relation to visits from these workers. Those who were visited infrequently were less likely to continue. Again, however, the trend was not significant.

As can be seen from Table 8.5, there was quite a strong association between the frequency of telephone contact and the likelihood of continuing. By and large, the more frequent the contact, the lower was the chance that the carer would leave. (Very frequent contact was associated with a greater chance of leaving, perhaps because it indicated a lack of confidence.)

This finding could reflect the support given by the family placement social workers or something about the attitude to fostering of the carers. (For example, committed carers could ring up more frequently.) At the least, it seems to be an index of the relationship between the two. It also raises the question of whether telephone contact might in selected cases maintain a good relationship without the necessity of frequent visits.

Table 8.5 Frequency of telephone contact and continuance		
Frequency of contact	n	Cease (%)
Once a week or more	166	21
Once every two weeks	204	14
Once a month	237	17
Less often	178	30
Never	11	46
Total	796	20

Source: General Questionnaire (excludes those with no link worker).
Mantel-Haenszel test for trend, Chi square = 7.81, df = 1, p = 0.0052.
Chi square = 21.49, df = 4, p = 0.0003.

In keeping with these findings those who stopped fostering gave their family placement social workers a significantly lower average support score than did those who continued (F = 5.135, df = 1, p = 0.0237) – see Table 8.6.

Table 8.6 Support from link worker and continuance		
Rating of support	*n*	Cease (%)
None	43	30
Some	308	23
A lot	459	17
Total	810	20

Source: General Questionnaire (excludes those with no link worker).
Mantel-Haenszel test for trend, Chi square = 6.72, df = 1, p = 0.0095.
Chi square = 6.74, df = 2, p = 0.0345.

Taken together, these findings strongly suggest that perceived support from the link worker is consistently associated with continuance.

Social worker visits and support

We asked the carers to rate the support given by the child's social worker. Leaving rates were comparatively high (30%) in the relatively few cases where the social worker was said to provide no support. However, rates of leaving were virtually identical in the next two categories ('some support' and 'a lot of support') and the differences were not significant.

We checked these conclusions against data from the sample of foster children. Children whose social workers had frequent contact with the carer were no more or less likely to be fostered by carers who ceased fostering. Similarly, children whose social workers were seen positively by carers (using a scale very similar to that which we used for link workers) were not more likely to have foster carers who ceased fostering.

So, in contrast to what we found with link workers, perceived social work support does not seem to relate to turnover.

Support from other professionals

The likelihood of continuing rose with the degree to which the carer felt supported by other professionals. Twenty-four per cent of those who reported no support from other professionals ceased caring. The comparable proportion for 'some support' was 20 per cent, and for 'a lot' was 15 per cent (p = 0.038).

Schools, GPs and others such as therapists or psychologists may provide support of this kind. It is a limitation of the General Questionnaire that we asked no questions about it.

Satisfaction with other aspects of social services

Satisfaction with other aspects of social services was unrelated to whether or not a carer continued. More specifically, there was no relationship between this outcome and reported satisfaction with:

- handling of allegations
- involvement in planning for foster child
- breaks
- information on previous foster children
- response out of office hours
- placement practice
- 'the support you get as a foster family'.

Nor was there any relationship between continuing and a global measure of satisfaction based on these variables.

Financial support

There were no significant relationships between continuing and carers' views of the generosity or otherwise of payments for foster care, of the equity of the financial arrangements, of the efficiency with which payments were handled or of the diligence of the authority in letting carers know of their entitlements.

By contrast, there was evidence that those receiving a larger income from fostering were less likely to leave. Carers who left reported an average fostering income of £121 per week. Those who stayed reported an income of £162 per week.

This difference is highly significant. However, it does not necessarily mean that higher income induces carers to stay. Income is strongly associated with the number of children a carer takes as well as with their ages. We have already seen that the number of foster children in a household is strongly associated with continuing to care.

As an immediate step, we computed the amount to which the carer's fostering income exceeded that which we would expect, given the number of children they took and their average ages (for this purpose we had to restrict the sample to those who were actually taking foster children at the time). We found that those who continued had on average a higher income than we expected.

We then divided the sample into four roughly equal groups, according to the amount their fostering income exceeded or fell short of what was predicted. As can be seen from Table 8.7, those whose income was 'a lot more' were less likely to cease fostering those whose income was less.

Table 8.7 Continuance and relationship between income and predicted income

| Status | Income in relation to predicted income | | | | Total |
	A lot less	Less	More	A lot more	
Continued	116 (80%)	118 (76%)	129 (84%)	138 (90%)	501 (82%)
Ceased	29 (20%)	33 (24%)	25 (16%)	16 (10%)	103 (18%)
Total	145 (24%)	151 (25%)	154 (25%)	154 (25%)	604 (100%)

Sources: General Questionnaire, Census 1 and Census 2.
Chi square for trend = 7.00, df = 1, $p = 0.008$. Chi square = 10.208, df = 3, $p = 0.017$.

Commitment to fostering

We assessed commitment to fostering through a series of statements with which the carers were expected to agree or disagree. As can be seen from Table 8.8, carers agreeing with statements that signified commitment to fostering were significantly more likely to continue with it.

Unsurprisingly, future intentions to give up fostering were strongly related to whether or not the carer did so. Half of those who said they would give up within two years had stopped fostering when followed up. The comparable percentage for those who said they might give up was 25 per cent, and for those who said they would not do so was 15 per cent. The number who left despite an original intention to continue was quite considerable. Indeed they constituted nearly half (47%) of all those who stopped fostering. As we will see in our next chapter, future and unpredicted events play an important role in final decisions to stop fostering.

Table 8.8 Commitment to fostering and continuance						
		% Ceasing to foster				
Statement	n	Strongly agree	Agree	Disagree	Strongly disagree	p
We get a lot of satisfaction from fostering	821	16	22	40	0 (n = 2)	0.0024
Fostering enriches our lives	804	15	21	29	22	0.0061
Everyone in this family is pleased we foster	804	18	18	32	27	0.0055

Source: General Questionnaire.

Note: All significance levels are based on a test for trend with 1 degree of freedom.

Housing

Continuing was unrelated to whether everyone in the household had a bedroom to themselves, to whether this situation was affected by fostering, or to the perceived beneficial, negative or mixed effect of foster care on the carer's housing.

Leisure

Continuing was unrelated to the perceived impact of fostering on leisure. Carers who perceived fostering as restricting their social lives were actually more likely to continue caring than others. This highly significant trend partly reflected the age of the children they fostered. Younger children are in some ways more restricting, but their carers are more likely to continue. However, the association remained when we took the average age of the foster children into account. Perhaps those who are prepared to have their leisure restricted are more committed to fostering and so more likely to continue.

Perceived impact on family relationships

Carers were more likely to continue if they perceived fostering as having had a good effect on family relationships, less likely to do so if they perceived it as having a mixed or neutral effect, and least likely to do so if they perceived the effect as negative. This apparent effect was significant for all carers taken together. Further analysis, however, showed that it was most significant where there were two or more adults in the family, where the proportions rose from 14 per cent through 19 per cent to 29 per cent ($p = 0.02$). Among lone carers there was no trend.

Strain

We compared those who continued and those who did not on their strain scores as measured by the *General Health Questionnaire*. Those who ceased fostering did score somewhat higher but the difference was small (3.6 as against 4.0) and only bordered on statistical significance ($p = 0.0553$).

The main influence here seemed to be how the carers interpreted their sense of strain. Where they said that the way they had been feeling had to do with fostering, there was a strong association with outcome. In these cases the average strain score was 6.76 for those who discontinued fostering as against 4.75 for those who continued. Where they did not attribute the way they had been feeling to fostering, the average strain scores were lower. Moreover, there was very little difference between the average scores of those who continued to foster (2.99) and of those who did not (3.19).[3]

Conclusions

As Triseliotis and his colleagues (2000) found in Scotland, the turnover of foster carers is not high – a figure of around 10 per cent a year seems to be correct. Our findings suggest that those who do leave do so for a variety of reasons. These include:

- *Personal reactions to fostering.* Those who got a lot of satisfaction from fostering tended to stay, as perhaps did those who were prepared to undergo social inconvenience. By contrast those who were under strain which they attributed to fostering were more likely to leave.

- *Social and social circumstances.* Older carers were more likely to cease fostering, as (for less obvious reasons) were younger ones, and lone carers lacking in informal support. Inactive carers were more likely to be working, possibly because getting a job was part of the transition from fostering.

- *Fostering situation.* Relative carers, and those fostering one older child, were more likely to leave. Those caring for a number of foster children or undertaking a number of roles were less likely to leave. The reason possibly related to a distinction between a commitment to fostering in general as against an individual child. Those fostering out of commitment to an individual would be likely to stop with the child's departure. This may explain the higher turnover among carers with older children. By contrast those fostering a number of children were less likely to leave. In these cases it was less likely that the departure of one child would 'clear the decks', leaving the carer with no foster child to whom they were obligated.

- *Formal support.* Perceived support from other carers, an income from fostering that was higher than predicted, above average levels of training, and the perceived supportiveness of family placement social workers and other professionals were all related to continuing.

In general, intentions to leave were related to doing so. Nevertheless, a high proportion of those who left had not intended to do so. This suggests that future unpredicted events might have a part to play in their decision. We test this hypothesis in our next chapter, where we examine the range of factors that may influence continuing or ceasing to foster.

Notes

1. Our questions about support asked for a rating of 'none', 'some' or 'a lot'. Among the lone carers, the trend for higher support to be associated with a lower likelihood of leaving was almost significant in relation to support from family (Mantel-Haenszel test for trend Chi square = 3.64, df = 1, $p = 0.0565$). It was significant in relation to support from relatives (Chi square = 4.20, df = 1, $p = 0.0404$).

2. The association between number of roles and continuing is not fully explained by the association of both with the number of children taken. We carried out a logistic regression with 'number of roles' and 'number of children fostered' as the independent variables and 'no longer fostering' as a dependent one. Both variables were associated with the outcome at a level of less than one in a thousand.

3. In this analysis, the association between strain and continuance was highly significant ($p<0.001$) as was the association between strain and how the carer interpreted it ($p<0.001$). The interaction (roughly speaking the degree to which strain was more strongly related to outcome when it was interpreted as arising from being a foster carer) was also very highly significant ($p<.0001$).

Chapter Nine

Explaining Outcomes:
Putting the Variables Together

Introduction

So far our analysis has focused on two variables at a time. This penultimate chapter provides some more complicated 'multi-variate' analysis.

The chapter has three main sections. In the first, we use tables to explore how combinations of variables appear to influence outcomes. In the second, we approach the same issue using rather more complicated statistical techniques (multiple and logistic regression) and a greater number of variables. In the third, we use our knowledge of subsequent events – specifically whether a placement disrupted – to see how far these, rather than initial conditions, explain whether carers continue caring or stop.

In carrying out these analyses, we have been guided by a small number of general hypotheses. Broadly, we explore the idea that a predisposition to continue fostering arises from a variety of factors including strain, attitudes to fostering, current family circumstances and financial inducement. Continuing in foster care reflects this predisposition, the ease with which carers can 'clear the decks' of their fostering responsibilities and – crucially – subsequent events. Schematically, these hypotheses can be set out as follows:

- informal support + no events → low strain

- low strain + formal support → positive view of fostering

- positive view of fostering + life stage + enhanced allowances → wish to stay

- wish to stay + initial fostering situation + no subsequent events
  → actually staying.

This model leaves a lot out. It says nothing about the love the carers may have for their foster children and the delight they can take in the children's jokes, affection and achievements. It also ignores the way a positive view of fostering is likely to reduce the sense of strain as well as reflect it. So much acknowledged, the ideas were able to guide our analysis. How far were the ideas borne out?

Some initial cross-tabulations

We first explored the kinds of relationship that might exist between our key variables. We focused on strain, attitude to fostering, intentions to leave and leaving. By using cross-tabulations we were able to have a clearer view of what was happening than would have been possible if we had begun with more complex analysis.

Strain and support

We defined the third of carers who scored highest on our 'strain score' as being 'under strain'. Our hypothesis was that carers would be more likely to be strained if they had relatively little support and experienced a relatively high number of 'negative fostering events'.

To explore this hypothesis, we first divided the carers into three equal groups: those who had experienced a relatively low number of events, those who had experienced a high number of events and those in the middle. We similarly distinguished between carers who said they did not get a great deal of informal support from any potential source (immediate family, relatives, friends, neighbours), those who said they did get this from one source and those who claimed such support from two or more groups.

One way to read Table 9.1 is to take each row in turn. As can be seen in each row the carers who had experienced a relatively low number of events were less likely to be strained than those who had experienced a medium number. These in turn were less likely to be strained than those who experienced a high number of events. Reading down the columns it is equally possible to see that those who experienced no significant support from any informal source were more likely to be stressed than those who experienced it from one, who in turn were more likely to be stressed than those who experienced it from two or more sources.[1] Again this is true of each column.

Table 9.1 Sources of support, events and per cent under high strain			
	Experience of events (%)		
No. of sources of support	Low	Medium	High
0	34	40	57
1	27	38	50
2 or more	23	29	35

Source: General Questionnaire – table based on 934 replies.

As an illustration of this point only 23 per cent of those with the highest degree of support and lowest experience of events were strained. The proportion strained among those with low support and a high experience of events was roughly two and a half times as great at 57 per cent.

Support and negative views of fostering

Table 9.2 illustrates a rather similar pattern. In this case, the percentages refer to the proportion of the sample that was in the 'worst' third in terms of their views of fostering. The potential sources of formal support were the family placement worker, field social workers, other professionals and other foster carers. Only 12 per cent of those with two sources of formal support and low strain had negative views. This contrasts with 53 per cent of those with high levels of strain and no sources of formal support.

Table 9.2 Sources of formal support, strain and 'negative' views of fostering			
	Levels of strain (%)		
No. of sources of support	Low	Medium	High
0	19	33	53
1	24	25	50
2 or more	12	17	45

Source: General Questionnaire – table based on 934 replies.

Our initial assumptions were that informal support would only affect views of fostering via its impact on strain. However, our analysis suggested that this was not the case. As can be seen from Table 9.3, a low level of informal support seems to go with negative views of fostering, even after levels of strain have been taken into account.

Table 9.3 Sources of informal support, strain and 'negative' views of fostering			
	Levels of strain (%)		
No. of sources of support	**Low**	**Medium**	**High**
0	25	31	66
1	20	17	43
2 or more	11	26	39

Source: General Questionnaire – table based on 941 replies.

Life stage and intentions to give up fostering

Our third set of hypotheses concerned the relationship between 'life stage' and intentions to give up fostering. As we have seen, some carers were happy to foster while it fitted their way of life – for example, while their children were at school and they wanted to be at home for them when they came back. Such carers might wish to stop fostering when their children left home, when they themselves might want to get a job. Alternatively, they might want to foster after their children had left but want to 'retire' when they reached their late fifties.

This view of fostering, as a limited 'life stage' commitment, suggests that carers may leave after a period of fostering, even though they have been happy about the experience. By contrast, they would presumably start caring in the belief that it fitted their current situation. At this point they would only think of leaving if they found they did not like it.

In our sample, attitudes to fostering did seem to be more strongly related to views about continuing in the first than in the second half of a fostering career (see Table 9.4). In the first half, they were associated with intentions to stop fostering. In the second stage they were not.

Table 9.4 Views of fostering, time fostering and intentions to leave		
	Time fostering (%)	
Views of fostering	Below median	Above median
Top third	1	9
Middle third	5	6
Lower third	9	12

Source: General Questionnaire – table based on 923 replies.

Leaving

We predicted that intentions of leaving would often be translated into action but would nevertheless be modified by the carer's situation. Carers who had a number of foster children would be less likely to lose all of them over a given period. Since they were committed to their children, they would also be less likely to leave, irrespective of their intentions to do so. As can be seen, Table 9.5 bears out this prediction.

Table 9.5 Number of foster children, intentions of stopping and percentage stopping			
	Stopping over next two years? (%)		
No. of foster children	Yes	Possibly	No
0	71	34	26
1	35	26	18
2 or more	40	19	10

Source: General Questionnaire – table based on 841 replies.

More complicated models

The tables presented thus far rely on very simple models of what it is that makes carers like fostering or decide to leave it. More complicated models have to rely on multi-variate analysis, which is more difficult to present. In what follows, we present some models of what it is that explains our outcome variables (strain, views of fostering, intentions to leave it and leaving it). The evidence discussed so far provides a number of factors that make it more likely that a foster carer will cease fostering, be stressed or have negative views towards it. Those we considered in our multi-variate analysis are set down below.

Basic characteristics
- Age – being over 55 or under 35.
- Couple status – being a lone carer without strong family support.
- Low degree of informal support.
- Whether working.
- Whether a relative.

Fostering situation
- Age of foster children – a high average age for foster children.
- Number of foster children – fewer than average taken.
- Fostered for above average length of time.
- Experienced an above average number of fostering 'events'.

Foster care support
- Income from fostering – lower than average and less than predicted.
- Training – fewer hours than average.
- Perceived support from other foster carers – lower than average.
- Support from link workers – lower than average.
- Support from social workers – lower than average.
- High satisfaction with breaks.
- High satisfaction with out-of-hours teams.

As described below, we did not use the last two variables in all our models.

Explaining strain

In our attempt to explain strain we used all these variables. We used 'backward selection' and multiple regression.

Table 9.6 Variables that predict strain			
Variable	Beta	t	p
Rating of support from family	-0.14	-3.03	0.001
Length of time fostering	-0.10	-2.58	0.010
Number of events	0.20	5.11	0.000
Satisfaction with breaks	0.12	-3.27	0.001
Support from social workers	-0.09	-2.47	0.014

Source: General Questionnaire.

To those unused to statistics these terms may explain little. Essentially we were trying to find the best or most efficient combination of variables for predicting strain. In selecting our combination we only included variables that made a statistically significant contribution to the overall prediction. To do this we began by looking at all the variables together, dropped the variable that made the least contribution and then ran the analysis again. This process continued until all the variables made a contribution.

As we have seen, satisfaction with breaks may be a misleading variable as it may or may not represent a rating based on experience of them. For this reason, we reran the model represented in Table 9.6 after omitting 'satisfaction with breaks' and the similar variable 'satisfaction with out-of-hours help'. The other variables remained in the equation at much the same level of significance.

The figures suggest that strain in foster care arises in part from:

- lack of support from family
- relatively brief experience of fostering
- experience of 'unpleasant events' (or the children who give rise to them)
- low support from social workers.

In interpreting the relationships between strain and support from family and social workers, it should be remembered that this could operate in either direction. Carers under strain may see their social worker as less supportive, or those who are less well supported may be under greater strain.

Table 9.7 Variables that predict attitudes to fostering			
Variable	Beta	t	p
Rating of support from family	0.14	1.99	0.047
Length of time fostering	0.16	3.68	0.000
Number of events	-0.17	-3.94	0.000
Being a lone carer	0.09	2.26	0.023
Support from link worker	0.13	3.61	0.003
Support from social workers	0.11	2.64	0.009
Support from other carers	0.08	1.98	0.048
Carer working	-0.09	2.21	0.028

Source: General Questionnaire.

Explaining the fostering score

Table 9.7 sets out a model explaining our view of the fostering score. The variables used in this model were the same as those used for Table 9.6, except that we omitted satisfaction with breaks and out-of-hours support.

In essence, the message of Table 9.7 seems to be that those who saw fostering in a positive light were more likely to see themselves as part of a team, supported by their family, social workers, family placement workers and other social workers. Satisfaction was also higher the longer the carer had been fostering and, at a much lower level of significance, if she was not working.

Intentions to leave or continue

Table 9.8 provides a model of intentions to leave or continue based on the same set of variables. There are two notable absentees from the list. The number of previous events was not related to future intentions to leave, although it was strongly related to having thought about this in the past.

Income was also unrelated to intentions. This is possibly because its effect was picked up by the variable 'number of foster children'. If 'number of foster children' is dropped from the analysis, predicted income becomes a strong predictor.

Table 9.8 Variables that predict intentions to leave or continue			
Variable	Beta	t	p
Number of sources of informal support	0.10	2.42	0.016
Length of time fostering	-0.20	-4.38	0.000
Number of foster children	0.17	4.11	0.000
Support from link worker	0.12	2.75	0.006
Support from social workers	0.09	2.22	0.027
Amount of training	0.10	2.29	0.022
Carer over 55	0.09	2.08	0.038

Source: General Questionnaire.

Inclusion of the average age of the foster children did not change the basic structure of the model. All the same variables appeared, with only slightly different significance levels but with average age added to the list.

Leaving

Actual departure reflected intentions to leave, the average age of the foster children and whether or not the carer was a relative. Carers who were relatives, who had older foster children and who had said they were thinking of leaving over the next two years were all more likely to stop. These variables were associated with leaving when put into the analysis together. In the case of average age the reason no doubt has partly to do with the greater likelihood that the children will leave either through disruption or because they are older and 'graduate' out of care. Relative carers will also be less likely than others to take further foster children once the related children have left.

Three other variables – support from other foster carers, more income from fostering than predicted and more training than average – were all significantly associated with leaving if considered on their own. However, these variables were significantly correlated with each other. Only one of them – support from other foster carers – was significantly associated with leaving when we put them into the analysis together. It seemed to us likely that the apparent good effect of support from other carers arose in part because it was, as it were, acting as proxy for the others. We therefore created a composite 'professional support score', formed by simply adding these variables together. As can be seen in Table 9.9, it was associated with leaving.

Table 9.9 Predictors of leaving foster care						
Predictor	Beta	S.E.	Wald	df	p	Exp (B)
Intention to leave	0.51	0.193	7.073	1	0.008	0.600
Average age of foster children	0.09	0.025	10.869	1	0.001	1.091
Relative carer	1.32	0.450	9.170	1	0.002	3.800
Professional support	-0.17	0.048	9.603	1	0.002	0.866

Source: General Questionnaire.

Events

In contrast to what we had predicted, carers who had experienced a high number of previous events were not more likely to leave than those who had not. As we noted before, the experience of events was strongly associated with thoughts of leaving in the past. The fact that past events are not associated with future behaviour suggests that the impact is relatively immediate. At the time, they predispose the carer to think of leaving foster care. Some may act on the thought. Those who continue may put the experience behind them and be no more likely to leave than anyone else.

Although previous events were not associated with ceasing to foster, subsequent events were. In the study of particular foster children, we were able to follow up 83 per cent through their foster carers. As will be apparent in the second report, there is room for disagreement over what counts as a 'disruption' – social workers, carers and link workers were not necessarily agreed over what had occurred. However, turnover was related to disruption irrespective of who defined it. In 22 per cent of the cases, at least one of the parties (social worker, link worker or carer) said that there had been a disruption. However, this was true of 60 per cent of the cases placed with carers who left foster care.

A rather more appropriate way of expressing these figures is in terms of the carers. The basic situation was as follows:

- Where a carer had a child who remained in the carer's placement he or she almost never left (only 3 out of 187 did so).

- The 168 carers who had no child in the sample with them at the end of the follow-up were more likely to leave themselves – a fifth did so.

- Among this latter group of carers, experience of disruptions was very strongly associated with leaving – 33 per cent of those experiencing a disruption left, as against only 11 per cent of the remainder (Chi square $= 12.44$, df $= 1$, $p<0.001$).

That children who remained in their placement had carers who remained there too is hardly surprising. It is almost true by definition. The three carers who left must have done so after our follow-up of the children finished.

The association between disruption and leaving among the remainder is striking. It is theoretically possible that the placements disrupted because the carer wanted to leave. In our view, this is very unlikely. In our questions we distinguished between disruptions and 'change in carer's circumstances'. Disruptions should not have been said to occur for reasons such as changes in job or carer moves. Moreover, there was no association between the occurrence of a disruption and whether or not the carer said they would or might leave over the next two years. So there was no evidence that carers who were likely to leave for other reasons were more likely to produce disruptions.

Twenty-one carers experienced a disruption but had another foster child in the sample who did not disrupt. None of these carers left. So it seems likely that the effects of disruptions lie in their combination of two circumstances. First, they turn the carer's mind to thoughts of leaving. We have already provided evidence for this in Chapter 6. Second, they may provide the circumstances in which a carer can stop fostering without letting down a foster child. It is only if this second condition is satisfied that disruption is associated with leaving.

Lack of numbers made it difficult to explain further why some carers left when their foster child did, and others did not. In part, no doubt, it had to do with the arrival and departure of foster children over the course of the study. Some of those who experienced a disruption will have had other foster children living with them, who arrived after the study started and of whom we had no knowledge. These carers will not have been in a position to stop caring when a child left.

Some evidence suggested that the reasons for leaving might be different when the carer experienced a disruption. Among those where there was no disruption, the professional involvement score was significantly associated with remaining, just as it was in the sample as a whole. Where there was a disruption, we could find no association between staying and any of our variables.

Conclusions

Reactions to fostering and decisions to leave it reflect the interplay of a variety of factors. It is unlikely that we have captured the relevant processes in all their detail. Nevertheless, some broad conclusions seem possible:

- The strains that arise from fostering reflect the difficult events that occur and the amount of support – particularly informal support – provided.

- Views of fostering reflect these strains and the support – particularly from family and social workers – that is available.

- Views of fostering, family circumstances, and the degree to which a carer receives a 'professional package' involving training, support from other carers and enhanced finance, all influence whether or not a carer thinks of leaving, with different weights probably being given to these factors, depending on the carer's situation.

- Whether a carer leaves depends partly on these views, partly on fostering circumstances (e.g. numbers fostered) and crucially on whether a placement breaks down and no other child is fostered at the time.

This analysis is, we believe, strongly consistent with the evidence of others, particularly Farmer and her colleagues (2002) and Triseliotis and his (2000). Its particular contribution lies in the additional evidence it provides of the importance of events. It also provides some pointers on what may be needed to reduce turnover of carers and increase retention. We deal with the possible implications in our final chapter.

Note

1. Table 9.1 illustrates the point. A regression equation using the strain score as a dependent variable and events and informal support as independent ones showed that both were related to strain ($p<0.001$ in both cases).

Chapter Ten

Conclusion

Introduction

It is time to take stock. In this concluding chapter we consider:

- the issues identified by the book
- findings relevant to these problems.

We also give recommendations, which are highlighted.

Issues

The most important and impressive feature of fostering is probably the commitment of the foster carers. Few of the 1528 carers – around one in ten over the course of the year – stopped fostering. The great majority said they found fostering enriching and satisfying. What they wrote gave as much evidence of the joys of fostering as of its inevitable problems. Problems, however, there are.

First, there is a lack of agreement on the roles foster carers should play and how they should be paid or recompensed. As others (Triseliotis *et al.* 2000; Waterhouse 1997) have found, different local authorities in the study approved carers for a very wide variety of different kinds of work under a bewildering variety of different titles. One authority seemed to have no 'official' long-stay carers, whereas in another, most carers were approved for long-stay care. Income from fostering varied widely and in ways that were only very roughly predicted from the ages and numbers of children the carer fostered. Around half of the carers agreed that the basis on which the authority rewarded carers was not fair.

Second, this variety is inevitably associated with pressure on the system. Variety brings specialisation and a greater likelihood that the precise specialty needed will not be available at the moment and in the place a vacancy is required. So there was evidence that a sizeable minority of carers (around a third) had taken children whom they thought unsuitable for their family. More commonly, children seemed to stay for long periods of time in placements that were officially short-term. There was some evidence of conscious or unconscious rationing by authorities under particular pressure. Increasing the number of children per placement or the number of foster carers taking children for whom they were not approved raised the capacity of the system. Ensuring that very few children stayed in foster care over the age of 17 reduced the pressure.

Third, foster care can damage carers' families. It is neither ordinary parenting nor an ordinary job. Unlike ordinary parents, foster carers may have to write reports on their children, discuss them with social workers, seek permission to have them spend a night away, calm down drunken or violent parents, attend courts, training or review meetings and face sadness when children they love move on. The children themselves may be difficult – stealing, lying, taking drugs, exposing themselves, staying out all night, leading other children astray and so on. Carers are exposed to painful events that disrupt family life and challenge their view of themselves as effective, caring people. Two-thirds of carers in our study had experienced one of our series of six major events – fostering breakdown, allegations, severe difficulties with birth parents, family tensions because of difficult placements, removal of children against their strong advice and other strong disagreements with the SSD. Those who had experienced such events were on average more stressed and more likely to leave.

The problems discussed above raise three inter-related questions:

- What different kinds of foster care are required?
- How can sufficient carers be recruited to undertake them?
- How can carers be supported to reduce strain and turnover?

What different kinds of foster care are required?

The categories under which carers were registered seemed to fall into five main types – relative, long-term, task-focused, short-term and respite. In addition, carers could be registered for more than one type – for example, short-term and long-term. These broad types differed from each other in such things as the ages and lengths of stay of the children.

This classification is far from original. Others have used similar ones – for example, long-term, intermediate, short-term (Berridge and Cleaver 1987; Triseliotis *et al.* 2000) or the slightly more elaborate classification suggested by Sellick and Thoburn (1996). Essentially, they provide a description of the situation as it is. This may or may not be what ought to be.

However, it is likely to reflect the needs fostering has to meet. For example, short-term foster care has grown up and survived because it is a logical response to certain kinds of family crisis.

As argued below, the question is not whether these kinds of foster care are needed, but rather how they should be thought about and supported. We discuss below the issues that seemed to us *raised by this study*. These are clearly not all the issues raised by particular forms of fostering. Moreover our discussion includes some evidence not presented in the main body of the book.

Relative foster care

Authorities varied in the proportion of relative carers included in the sample. (Appendix 3 provides more detail on this group.) In the four authorities where sufficient relatives were included for analysis, they differed consistently from other carers. On average they were less materially well off. Commonly they quarrelled with the child's parent(s), either because of strains arising because they fostered or because they had never got on well. On average they received less money for fostering than predicted from the number or ages of their foster children. They received very little training – much less than other carers. They were visited less frequently by family placement workers and were significantly less likely to say they had much support from them.

The carers did not necessarily resent these arrangements. They were more likely than others to see their income from fostering as generous, less likely to see the basis for payment as unfair, and more likely to say they would continue without any income from fostering at all. Typically, they felt the family placement social worker visited enough. Overall, they were as satisfied with the support they received as any other carer. They were, however, less satisfied with the amount of training they had received, and with its quality and relevance if they had received any. More detailed analysis showed that their attitudes to training and support were not homogeneous. Some defined themselves as primarily relatives and wanted as little to do with formal arrangements as possible. Others felt that they were foster carers and entitled to the same training, support and allowances as carers who were not relatives.

We shall see in the next book that the placement of children with relatives was not more successful than placement with 'ordinary' carers. If anything, it was less successful, although the problems it raised tended to be different. As others have argued (Broad 1999; Wheal 1999), there needs perhaps to be greater clarity over when children placed with relatives should be treated as fostered. If they are to be included in the system they should, presumably, be entitled to the same support as other carers. As Wheal (1999) has pointed out, they have certain needs. These include information on entitlements, their obligations as foster carers, and the problems they are likely to meet in fostering related children.

> There is considerable scope for expanding the number of relative carers. At present the proportion of foster children is far lower than it is, for example, in some states in the USA or in Australia. Relative fostering is not, however, a free good and has problems of its own. Authorities should think through their policies on relative fostering – when it should be used, how it should be financially supported, and what training and support it requires. In forming these policies they should be aware that relative carers differ from others and are not themselves a homogeneous group. These issues can be dealt with in various ways. Our own views have been set out elsewhere (Sykes *et al.* 2002).

Long-stay foster care

Authorities varied in the proportion of carers registered as 'long-stay'. One had no carers in this category. Nevertheless, all authorities provided long-stay care, in the sense that some children were fostered for considerable lengths of time by the same carer.

The *de facto* existence of long-stay foster care probably reflects the need for it. As we will see in the next two books, not all children can go home. More children might be adopted – it is certainly true that some authorities have more adoptions than others. However, the lengthy delays in finding suitable adopters for even young children suggest that the scope for placing older children is not great, even if they want it. International comparisons quoted in the Prime Minister's review of adoption (Department of Health 2000) support this view. Proportionately more children are adopted out of care in England (4%) than anywhere else except the USA (6.6%), which makes more use of foster care adoptions.[1]

So the implication is that long-stay fostering is here to stay. The problem is not to do away with it but rather to think through its implications. How should long-stay carers be financially supported? In some authorities, carers whom we classified as 'long-term' seemed to get more than the average paid to carers fostering the same number of children of similar age. In other authorities they got less. Is it right, as seems to have been the case in one of our authorities, that fostering should virtually cease by the age of 17? What should be the arrangements for dealing with the small number of severely disabled children when they reach the age of 18 and are no longer covered by the foster care regulations? Should there be more encouragement for foster carers to keep in touch with former long-stay children and to allow others to stay on over the age of 18? What help might they need to do this?

> Authorities should think through their policies on long-stay fostering, should agree that it is needed and should answer the questions raised above. These are issues dealt with in more detail in our projected third book that discusses what happened to the 596 foster children over three years.

Task-focused foster care

One authority classified almost all its carers as 'project carers'. It was not obvious what the distinction was between these carers and 'mainstream' carers elsewhere. Other authorities had a small number of carers who were on special schemes and were expected to take particularly difficult children. We were not at all satisfied with our ability to distinguish between these carers and others.

In this, we perhaps reflected the situation on the ground. Foster care is predominantly conceived as a way of looking after children rather than changing them. Foster carers may attract extra money or support because they look after particularly difficult children. Distinctions between carers are commonly made in terms of the difficulty of the children whom they look after. However, the pressure on places means that very difficult children may be placed with a wide variety of carers. Distinctions are blurred as a result.

Our own view is that treatment foster care should be developed. The virtual demise of residential care has left a gap in arrangements aiming to provide therapy. American models of therapeutic fostering exist (Chamberlain 1998; Clark et al. 1994; Hill et al. 1999).

These models should be tested in the UK. A promising step towards doing this has already been made (Walker *et al.* 2002) and the Department for Education and Skills is encouraging experiments in it.

Short-stay and mixed foster care

The difficulty of drawing sharp boundaries between different kinds of foster carers was apparent in other ways. Just under a third of carers seemed to be registered for mixed categories of caring (e.g. short and long). Foster children with short-stay foster carers had already stayed on average for 12 months. (The average stay for the longest-staying child in such households was 15 months.) This situation reflects the difficulty of finding closely matched placements for children. Social workers have to wait until an appropriate placement becomes available. Matters may be eased by an increase in the numbers of carers. Unless, however, authorities are prepared to allow and fund a large number of vacant placements, the problem will not disappear.

So again the issue is that of recognising and thinking through a situation that is inevitable. In practice, those who were registered for more than one role were less likely to stop fostering than others. This was partly because they took, on average, more foster children and were thus less likely to have a space when they had no foster children and could cease fostering. However, they were less likely to cease fostering than others who took similar numbers of children. Most probably, the number of roles for which they were registered reflects their commitment in the first place, arising, for example, because they were willing to extend a short-stay placement into a long one because of their affection for a child.

Authorities should accept the need for placements that are able to take a wide variety of children on a short- or a reasonably long-term basis. They should recruit carers for these placements directly but also through responding to the wishes of carers recruited for short-term roles. Some of these should attach to children who need to stay for longer periods.

How can foster care be made more attractive?

We suggested earlier that pressure on foster care places could not be completely removed by any conceivable increase in the number of carers. This is not to say that an increase in carers would not help. Clearly it would.

An increase should also be feasible. Special schemes have proved attractive to black and Asian carers (Caesar *et al.* 1994). Some authorities have more children fostered per head than others. Presumably they have more carers. Others have significantly increased their numbers of foster children. Presumably they have also managed to increase their number of carers. Lessons from these successes might be applied to the recruitment of white carers and in more authorities.

> Two general lines of approach to recruiting more carers seem promising. The first would involve paying attention to the reasons why certain families are not involved in fostering – what we call later 'situational constraints' – and trying to counter them. The second would involve giving carers more money and support.

Attending to the situational constraints on fostering

One striking finding is that the social characteristics of foster carers have changed little over the years. There has, it is true, been a change in the number of childless couples. This probably reflects the changed view of fostering that is no longer seen as a form of quasi-adoption. In other ways, our results are very close to those of Bebbington and Miles (1990), Gray and Parr (1957) and Triseliotis and his colleagues (2000) in Scotland. Compared with the general population, foster care families are more likely to involve two parents, only one of whom goes out to full-time work, less likely to have two or more children under five and more likely to contain a woman aged between 30 and 55 (Bebbington and Miles 1990).

These characteristics imply that the supply of foster carers will be higher in authorities that have many families of this kind than in those that do not. The local employment situation may be particularly relevant. Areas where there is high female employment provide fewer carers (Moralee 1999). Male carers have a relatively high unemployment rate both in Triseliotis and his colleagues' study (2000) and in ours. So it may be that the income from fostering becomes more attractive when the chance of acquiring income from employment is less.

Further evidence for the situational constraints on fostering comes from our findings on who continues and who does not. Families with children under five, lone carers, carers under the age of 35 and carers over the age of 55 were all less likely to continue (in the case of children under five, the association was not significant through small numbers). Active carers in work were no less likely to continue than others. However, inactive carers were more likely to be working. This suggests that some carers become 'inactive' in order to get work. So, in general, the factors that distinguish carers from the general population are also related to whether or not they continue in foster care.

These findings suggest that those who seek to increase the supply of foster carers should think first of what is likely to constrain carers from applying or would make it difficult for them to foster if they start. Relevant factors include housing, the situation of carers for young children or as a lone parent, a possible need or wish to work, and age.

HOUSING

Some carers in our study complained about the reluctance of authorities to help with housing improvements and extensions. In the view of the carers, help with this would have enabled them to take more foster children or care better for the ones they had.

In our second and third books we argue that the number of children in a placement is certainly a crucial issue for individual children. It was not, however, a factor that affected all children the same way. Some children reacted to the presence of others by feeling excluded and neglected. Others liked 'mothering' younger children or got support from the carers' children or their 'foster siblings'. On average the number of children in the placement made no apparent difference to the outcome of the placement either way.

> With appropriate safeguards, a greater willingness to help in this way might expand the number of children fostered.

YOUNG PARENTHOOD

It is not clear why young parents foster less than older ones. Those that do foster seem on the whole to foster younger children. Difficulties in managing toddlers together, or in timetabling days or managing part-time work when one child is at school and another not, may explain some of the problem. Carers may also be understandably reluctant to have children of an age that they have not yet experienced with their own. Whatever the reason, carers of this age who fostered children older than their own were more likely to leave.

> Reassurances over the age of children placed with younger carers might attract more of them to fostering.

LONE CARERS

Lone carers seemed to be particularly dependent on family support. One local authority has invited carers to recruit friends or relatives as relief carers who can be registered with the authority to provide them with a break when needed (Sellick, personal communication).

> The key to recruiting more lone carers could well be schemes which either made it easier for them to receive this support or effectively substituted for it (e.g. through arrangements which enabled the carer to work).

CARERS WHO WANT TO WORK

Foster care might be made more attractive to carers who want to work.

> Attracting carers who want to work could involve treating foster care as work (e.g. in terms of pay, holidays, pension), making it easier to combine foster care with work (e.g. by holiday schemes) or ensuring that caring attracted qualifications and training that made it a stepping stone to field or management roles in social services.

OLDER CARERS

Older carers were thinking of giving up caring for reasons of health and age. Some felt that they lacked the energy to do more than 'see out' the children they had with them at the time. One suggested that, if offered the opportunity, she would like to undertake less strenuous forms of caring – for example, respite caring or leading support groups for carers.

> Involving older carers in less full-time roles (e.g. training or the provision of short breaks) could be a useful way of employing their expertise and extending their career as carers.

Recruitment arrangements

Our study did not deal directly with recruitment arrangements. It did, however, provide indirect support to the views of Triseliotis and his colleagues (2000) that experienced carers should be involved in them. Carers in our study were strongly committed to caring and could speak with authority on its joys as well as its difficulties. They can surely play a positive role in recruitment as, according to our respondents, they do in training.

This suggestion is not intended to reduce the part played by family placement workers in recruitment. These too were greatly appreciated by carers. They have the skill and experience to discuss with carers the difficulties there might be in fostering in their particular situation. By exploring how these difficulties might be overcome, they should reduce the situational constraints on fostering discussed above.

According to Triseliotis and his colleagues (2000), very few of those who register an interest in caring actually become carers. Increasing this proportion would increase numbers and reduce the cost per carer recruited. It is an area where further research and experiment is needed.

> Experiments in recruitment could well focus on the time after serious enquiries have been made, the use of carers in recruitment and the use of family placement social workers in helping would-be carers to think through potential difficulties.[2]

Paying more for fostering

Our evidence is also indirectly relevant to the effects of income from fostering on the supply of carers. Other studies (Leat 1990; Oldfield 1997) suggest that allowances are a financial necessity for some carers, but that average allowances are low relative to what a foster child actually costs.[3] So it is not surprising that local authorities pay more for foster care where the supply of foster carers is likely to be low relative to need (Bebbington and Miles 1990; Moralee 1999) – a fact which suggests that they have found this necessary to increase their number of carers.[4] Authorities that pay relatively low rates have greater difficulties over vacancies (Waterhouse 1997). Somewhat dated American evidence (Simon 1975) suggests that authorities that pay more for carers tend to have more of them.

Our own study suggested that income from fostering played various roles in enabling it. For some it was a necessity. For some it was (or more often should have been) a fair recognition of a job well done. For some it was a bonus – something that enabled them to do work they enjoyed and/or which fitted in with their family arrangements and their view of the income they could command. For many it was all these things at once.

Overall, 60 per cent of carers agreed that without an income from fostering they could not continue. Those who were better educated were less likely to say this – presumably they were better off and could more easily afford to foster. Those who had more and older foster children, and whose costs would therefore be higher, were more likely to see allowances as a necessity. An adequate maintenance allowance is clearly a necessity if poorer families are not to be excluded from fostering altogether.

Perceptions of the generosity of payments varied. Probably they reflected carers' experiences of fostering and the alternatives they saw being available to them. Those who felt fostering should be paid as a job (75% did), who were better educated and so probably in a position to get a better paid job, or who already had a job, were all less likely to see the payments as generous. So too were those who saw fostering as having a bad effect on their family. By contrast, those who saw fostering as having a good effect on their family were more likely to see the allowances favourably.

This suggests the obvious point that the importance and attractiveness of the income from fostering will vary with the carer's circumstances. Some, notably relatives, but also those who respond to advertisements for named children, foster because of their commitment to these particular children.[5] Others are family-minded. They value a job which fits in with their family commitments, brings in some money and allows them to use their love of children and parenting skill. Yet others see fostering as a challenging, professional job. The obvious comparisons are with adoption, child minding and residential work, and the importance of enhanced allowances might be expected to vary accordingly.

These distinctions between different kinds of carer are, in practice, blurred. For example, although relative carers are more likely than others to feel that the income from fostering is 'generous' and the basis for it fair, they are only slightly less likely to feel that it should be paid as a job. However, the differences suggest that enhanced allowances should in part be based on what the authority is entitled to expect of a carer. For example, it is probably unfair to expect that a carer who is caring in part because it fits her family commitments should take in a very difficult child who may disrupt the family. These reduced expectations could reasonably be reflected in reduced enhancement.

Overall, our findings add to the accumulating evidence that financial incentives have an impact on carers. Those who got more income from fostering than would have been expected from the ages and number of their foster children saw the benefits as more generous. They were also less likely to quit fostering.

> A substantial increase in the number of carers will almost certainly require an increase in the money paid to them. At the moment, the risk is a decrease in the number, as competition from the independent sector drives up rates and decreases the ability of local authorities to pay the carers they have.

The implications for the way enhanced payments should be distributed are less clear. To us, they suggest a system of payment based on what can be expected of carers rather than on their skills or the difficulty of a particular child.[6] At present, there are very wide variations between authorities in the money paid. We found substantial variation within authorities in the payments received by carers taking similar numbers and ages of child. About half the carers felt that the basis for calculating payments was unfair.

> A clear, widely understood, national scheme for calculating payments should help reduce this sense of unfairness.

How can carers be better supported?

Money on its own is not the key to improving foster care. For many carers, the amount paid does not defray the true costs of caring. They do not foster for money. Even if they did, there would be easier ways of earning a living. Moreover, a higher income from fostering was associated with greater strain, presumably because it went with more difficult children. It was also abundantly clear that although fostering could bring great fulfilment, it could also be destructive. Carers and their families could pay a heavy price for their altruism, and this price needs to be reduced.

To judge from our study three principles are likely to be particularly important in achieving this end.

First, the kind of fostering the family is asked to undertake needs to be related to its capacity and situation. As argued earlier, families in different situations are likely to face particular difficulties in fostering. These potential difficulties need to be appreciated and taken into account. In addition, carers feel they are suited to different kinds of children. Some like a challenge, some want to give love, some want teenagers, some babies and so on. In general, these preferences do seem to be taken into account. However, carers often felt that they had not been given the information they needed before deciding to take a child (see our second book). This is perhaps in some cases understandable, but nevertheless undesirable.

Second, carers are likely to need a combination of support and to be treated as part of the 'social services team'. At a minimum this involves adequate allowances, training, support from other carers and support from family placement social workers. As argued above, financial support on its own is not enough. The combination of support just given seems the one most likely to enable carers to continue. Arguably, it allows them to see themselves as part of a professional team. They are no longer isolated parents financially worse off than if they had not fostered, while facing challenges they had not expected and which no one they know well is in a position to understand.

Third, carers need services to provide a flexible and supportive response to events.[7] The events we list seem to be occupational hazards of fostering. Two-thirds of carers had been exposed to at least one of them. Breakdowns are by far the most common and are strongly associated with carers ceasing to foster. Aldgate and Hawley (1986) argue that these crises might be pre-empted by early intervention (see Quinton *et al.* 1998 and our second book) and also that foster carers need support in coming to terms with them. This study would support this view. It also supports the need to develop practice in relation to allegations (Calder 1999; Hicks and Nixon 1991). Other events (e.g. family crises associated with fostering) are also painful and call for support if possible.

These basic points can be supplemented by a number of more detailed ones that relate to particular aspects of practice.

Financial arrangements

Late payments and inefficiency in informing carers of their financial entitlements, dealing with payments for breakages, transport for the foster child and so on seem to be among the 'hassles' of fostering. There appear to be quite wide variations between authorities in these respects, with one authority in our study being seen in a much worse light in this respect than others. Efficiency over financial arrangements requires good information for social workers, slick procedures and no doubt much else besides.

The financial arrangements should be monitored and, where necessary, improved.

Out-of-hours duty teams

Out-of-hours duty teams were commonly seen as out of touch with fostering. It was also alleged that they put off dealing with problems rather than tackling them on the spot. Those who were most likely to have contact with these teams were the most dissatisfied with them. However, there were differences between authorities in the degree of satisfaction with the arrangements.

Carers' opinions of them should be monitored. Improvements should then be made where necessary.

Relief breaks

Not all carers wanted relief breaks and some refused them on principle. Nevertheless, others found them a lifeline. Again, there seemed to be differences between authorities in the degree of satisfaction with relief breaks.

> Carers' views of relief breaks should be monitored. Improvements should then be made where necessary.

Carers' groups

Not all carers wanted to go to carers' groups and not all areas had them. In rural areas they could be difficult to organise. Those who went to them regularly seemed to find a lot of support from them. They were certainly a means whereby carers got to know other carers and were able to seek support from them on an individual basis.

> All areas should offer carers' groups or an alternative to them (e.g. internet-based support groups) if they present practical difficulties.

Training

Training was appreciated. Carers wanted more of it. The more they got, the more likely they were to stay. The relationship was not necessarily causal. Keen carers may have been more likely to apply for training. However, there is every reason to make training as good as possible.

Carers wanted more involvement of experienced carers in training. They would also have liked more attention to topics which were relevant to the particular age group of their foster children, and which they might not have met through their experience of parenting. They also wanted more attention to the difficulties of attending training (e.g. work or care commitments).

We shall see in our second book that training was not associated with improved outcomes for children. This is not an argument against it. It is an argument for providing a stronger rationale for the kind of training provided, using the experience of effective carers in providing training, and evaluating the results.

> Training is essential. More attention should be paid to carers' views in providing it. Potentially effective courses should be evaluated for their effects on outcomes.

Social work practice

Carers generally praised their social workers. They appreciated workers who sorted practical problems, listened to what they said, mediated between them and the child, understood the child and dealt well (in the carer's view) with the child's family and with other agencies. However, they complained of social workers who did not respect their views, failed to provide them with information, were continually in meetings, sick or on courses, did not return telephone calls, undermined (in the carer's view) the carer's discipline and did not do what they said they would.

> Carers' views of social workers should be monitored at a general level. Improvements should then be made where necessary. What carers want from social workers is analogous to what all clients want – warmth, efficiency, respect, reliability and straightforwardness. These qualities should be key themes in selecting and training social workers.

Practice by family placement social workers

Carers gave great praise to family placement social workers. Complaints, if any, were similar to those made of social workers, but they were rare. The main issue was infrequent visiting. Family placement social workers who visited more frequently were more highly rated by carers. Frequent telephone contact was also associated with appreciation and with carers continuing to foster. It may be that this reflects carer 'keenness' rather than social work supportiveness. The more committed they were, the more often they rang the social worker. However, it raises the question of how much support could be provided by telephone.

> An increase in telephone support would free time for other things. This possibility should be explored with carers and tried out on an experimental basis.

Placement endings

Placement endings can be very painful to carers who have become very fond of the children involved.

> This pain should be acknowledged more often than it is. Use should be made of the 'emotional capital' accumulated through the relationship (e.g. by encouraging ongoing contact where appropriate). Wherever possible, carers should be given the opportunity to learn of the progress of their former foster children.

Events

Placement breakdowns and other events were painful, and caused carers to re-evaluate whether they would go on. Support at these points might reduce the loss of carers and enable those unsuited to caring to move on with less hurt.

> Placement breakdowns should always lead to a discussion between at least the carer and the family placement social worker about what went wrong and what lessons might be learnt for the future.

Monitoring carer turnover

Authorities did not routinely monitor the turnover of their carers so that it could be compared with figures for other authorities. In practice, this would have been difficult to do. There were different degrees of willingness to take inactive carers off the list. This meant that the base figure and the number leaving were both difficult to compare across authorities.

A problem with such figures is that they are now interpreted in the context of league tables and bring with them a natural desire to cheat. In our view, they are essential management information, necessary both for planning and for monitoring carer morale.

> Definitions of turnover should be agreed and appropriate figures collected without the implication that some authorities are 'doing better' than others.

Learning lessons from special schemes

Walker and her colleagues (2002) have recently reported on the outcomes of a scheme for fostering Scottish children who would otherwise have been in secure accommodation. In this scheme carers had very regular support from their own social worker, regular meetings involving, at the minimum, their own social worker, the child's social worker and the foster child, guaranteed arrangements for respite and a dedicated out-of-hours service. They were regarded as professionals and paid a salary. The young people were rarely placed in a rush and carers were not pressurised into taking those whom they thought unsuitable for their household. Despite the difficult nature of the clientele no carer left over the three years of the scheme's operation.

As can be seen the scheme appears to have put into operation key elements of the support package recommended earlier. There is now a considerable body of research that bears on these issues and the findings are unusually consistent. It seems that we do know what to do in order to support carers. Over the years there has almost certainly been a great advance in putting these lessons into effect. The turnover of carers is now much less than seems to have been the case in the 1970s. There remains, however, much to do.

> Authorities should study the lessons of the Scottish scheme and see how far they can put them into effect.

Conclusions

Foster care provides an outstanding example of community altruism. It does not, however, offer a blank cheque. Foster carers provide care in the context of their own lives and because of their commitment to individual children. They stop fostering because it no longer fits their lives, because of poor support or devastating experiences or because of the departure of children to whom they are committed. They need support that respects their family contexts, their commitment and their skill. They need efficient handling of their practical issues and a prompt and sympathetic response to their emergencies. Their support requires money, training and clarity of policy and procedure. Foster care is not a free good but it is a remarkable one.

Notes

1. The text states that these proportions reflect 'percentage of children adopted from care' – it is not clear what this is a percentage of (e.g. adoptees, entrants to the care system, those there at any one time). Assuming the base is comparable, England clearly does 'well'.

2. No doubt they do so. However, the literature on their role in recruitment seems pre-occupied with the need to weed out ineffective or risky carers.

3. This statement blurs distinctions between the cost of a child, the cost of a foster child (which is more) and the indirect costs of caring (e.g. loss of opportunity to work). See Oldfield (1997).

4. These authorities may be in urban areas such as London where competition between authorities for carers may also increase rates.

5. Our finding that carers generally wait until they have no resident children before they stop fostering suggests that commitment to individual children becomes a motive for most.

6. Expectations imply the kind of child who may be placed and hence the skills needed. As criteria, they could avoid the need to penalise success by lowering payment as children improved, stigmatising children by implying that better paid carers always had 'worse' children' or implying that a carer's value was strongly related to measurable skills.

7. Triseliotis and his colleagues (2000) found rather sharper differences than we did in the way carers who left viewed support from social services. This study compared carers who had left with others who stayed. Views may have crystallised because of the crises associated with leaving.

Sample Representativeness

Introduction

The study was carried out in seven authorities selected to provide social and organisational diversity and to be reasonably accessible to the research team. Two are London boroughs (one inner, one outer), two are urban unitary authorities, one is a metropolitan borough with a rural hinterland, and the remaining two are large and diverse shire counties. Three of the authorities have sizeable minority ethnic populations, a fact which is reflected in the ethnic composition of their foster carers.

The prime purpose of the study was to identify the effects of support. For this reason, the representativeness of the samples is probably a less key consideration than it would be if the aim was to describe. It is possible that the association between support and, say, ceasing to be a foster carer is different among those who respond and those who do not. This, however, is only the case if quite complicated assumptions hold good. By contrast, a lack of representativeness in, say, the proportion of carers from minority ethnic groups who respond could distort estimates of the true proportion both of minority ethnic carers themselves and of other characteristics with which they are associated.

The aim of this appendix is to give a sense of the biases that may exist in our sample. It considers:

- the degree to which the authorities are representative of childcare practice nationally
- the degree to which those responding to the postal questionnaire represent carers in the authorities.

Chapter 3 of this book and Chapter 2 of the second book consider how far the foster children in the study are nationally representative.

Representativeness of authorities

We compared our authorities with the national figures for 1998 on the characteristics given below.

Tables A1.1 and A1.2 compare the rates of looked-after children estimated from national statistics for our seven authorities and compare them with the figures for England as a whole. As can be seen, the figures are very close.

Table A1.1 Looked-after children: rates for England and sample authorities		
Rate per 10,000 children	England	Sample authorities
Looked after on 31 March	47	48
Started being looked after in 1998	26	25
Ceased being looked after in 1998	26	26

Source: Department of Health statistics: *Children Looked After by Local Authorities: Year Ending 1998*. Tables 3 and 4.

Table A1.2 Type of placement for looked-after children: England and sample authorities		
Type of placement	England %	Sample authorities %
Foster	66	68
Children's home	12	10
With parents on order	10	11
Placed for adoption	5	5
Other placement	7	7
Three or more placements[a]	19	23
Two years in same placement or placed for adoption[b]	51	50

Source: Department of Health statistics: *Children Looked After by Local Authorities: Year Ending 1998*. Tables 9 and 10.
[a] Percentage calculated using those in care system for four years or more as base.
[b] Information not available for all authorities.

Census

The census consisted of all those foster carers registered with the seven authorities with two exceptions: child minders who had been registered as foster carers only so that they could look after the children overnight if necessary were excluded, as were a very small number of foster carers where the local authority had requested us to do so because it was taking disciplinary proceedings against them. The potential sample after these exclusions was 1528.

Ninety-three per cent of the forms for Census 1 were returned. Those that were not were almost entirely concentrated in one area of one authority. The response for Census 2 at follow-up was better – 97 per cent. We see no reason to think that either sample is seriously biased by the response rate. It is possible, however, as discussed in the text, that we missed relative foster carers who were dealt with by area teams. Our sample contains a comparatively low proportion of relative carers compared with national figures.

General Questionnaire survey response rate

All the foster carers in Census 1 were eligible for the General Questionnaire survey and were sent a questionnaire. The overall response rate was 61 per cent. This is respectable by the standards of postal questionnaires, but is less important in itself than whether the sample is biased, in the sense that some carers are more likely to respond than others.

We compared respondents and non-respondents on the information provided in the census. The pro-formas covered the factors we thought likely to influence response. The main variables that were related to response were:

- local authority (from a low of 40% in the two London boroughs to a high of 71% in a shire county)
- whether the carer was active (65% as against 45% where the carer was not fostering and not expected to do so again)
- age of eldest foster child (from 75% where the child was aged under two to 58% where the young person was 16 or more)
- whether the carer had other paid work (58% where this was so, to 65% where it was not).

Carers who were said to describe themselves as not of British origin were significantly less likely to respond (44% as against 65%). This association was partly, but not wholly, explained by the fact that the majority of these carers were in the London boroughs, where the response rate was low among all respondents. Outside London, there was a very low response rate among the small number of Asian carers,[1] a somewhat (but not significantly) lower response rate among black carers, and a slightly higher response rate among the very small number of 'dual heritage' respondents. If all minority ethnic clients were combined, there was no difference in the response rate within London (indeed, minority ethnic carers were slightly more likely to respond than others). Outside London, the difference was just significant, with fewer minority ethnic carers returning their questionnaires (53% as against 67%).

The most serious potential source of bias is, in our opinion, the relatively low response rate among London authorities. Compared with other carers, those in London received much more income from fostering and were much more likely to come from ethnic minorities. In other ways they seemed to differ little. Thus, they were no more or less likely to leave and did not differ on their attitudes to fostering. Any differences that did exist seemed to reflect the much higher proportion of ethnic minorities among these carers (68% of those in the London authorities as against 5% among the four authorities where we asked this question elsewhere). This difference in the proportion of minority ethnic carers 'explained' other differences between London and other authorities – notably, differences in the proportion of lone carers (45% in the London authorities as against 20% in the others).

A second source of bias is that carers who were likely to perceive themselves as centrally involved in the business of foster care were more likely to respond. Thus, response rates were relatively low among 'inactive carers' (45%), relative carers (44%) and 'specific carers' (i.e. carers who were recruited to foster a specific child: 45%). Conversely, there was a relatively high response rate among those whose registration was described as 'mainstream' (76%). The main dangers of these potential sources of bias are:

- We may underestimate the key importance of issues relating specifically to ethnic minorities in the London boroughs.

- An important example of this is the proportion of lone carers with their particular needs for support.

- We may overestimate the degree of 'professionalisation' among carers by giving less than due representation to those whose primary allegiance is to specific foster children, rather than to the profession of foster care itself.

Readers should bear these points in mind. We do not consider that the other sources of bias (age of foster child and outside paid work) are sufficiently large to have a serious impact on our conclusions.

Note

1. Our questionnaire was in English but we included an offer in other languages to arrange for a translator to visit if necessary. This offer was not taken up, so this part of our strategy was not effective.

Census Pro-forma

Identification number of foster carer				
Type of fostering for which approved: *(e.g. long-term, relative etc.)*				
Is this family				*Circle one number only*
	currently fostering?			1
	If 'yes', how many children?			
	waiting for a new foster child?			2
	'inactive' as foster carers?			3
Age of eldest child currently fostered				*Circle one number only*
	0–1	1	16+	5
	2–4	2	Don't know	6
	5–9	3	Not applicable	7
	10–15	4		
Estimated educational level of foster carer *(please estimate for most educated carer)*				*Circle one number only*
	Degree/Professional			1
	A level/skilled trade (e.g. NNEB)			2
	O level/GCSE			3
	None of the above			4
	Can't say			5

Does the main foster carer have other paid work?	*Circle one number only*	
	Yes, full-time	1
	Yes, part-time	2
	No	3
Self-ascribed ethnicity	*Circle one number only*	
	Asian	1
	Black	2
	Mixed	3
	White British	4
	White other	5
	Don't know	6

Kinship Carers

Just under 7 per cent of our sample were said by the family placement social workers to be relative carers. Other relative carers in the census were apparently included under other headings (e.g. long-term carers). Among those carers replying to the postal questionnaire, 71 (8%) said that they only fostered a child related to them. Thirty-three of these relative carers had not been previously identified as such in the census. So it seems that the figure of 7 per cent from the census is an underestimate. A truer figure may well be around 13 per cent of the census (15% of the active carers). Those who were identified as relative carers were less likely to return their questionnaires (44% v. 63%).

These various sources of potential bias suggest caution in drawing conclusions from the sample. One or two carers returned our questionnaires to us saying that it did not seem to apply to them as they were really relatives. Our sample may therefore contain an unrepresentatively high number of carers who identified themselves as foster carers. Some of these clearly felt that they were not properly recognised as such. That said, our data on relative carers seemed worth reporting as a contribution to the literature (e.g. Broad 2001b; Waterhouse and Brocklesbury 1999). The following information is reported at greater length in an article (Sykes *et al.* 2002).

As a group, kinship carers in the study were similar in age and ethnicity to others. They were, however, more disadvantaged. They were more likely to have an unemployed partner (43% v. 20%) and more likely to be seen as having no educational qualifications (67% v. 37%). In certain respects they were less well supported. They were twice as likely as others to say that they got no support from their immediate family (16% v. 7%). These difficulties were exacerbated by a very common tendency for quarrels to arise within their family, tensions that had either pre-existed the placement or arose because of it. Difficulties over contact were common, with family members feeling they could drop in at will – something which the relative carer might be expected to control.

Despite these difficulties kinship carers received on average less formal support. They were much more likely to have received no training (57% as against 5%), less likely to have a link or family placement social worker (5% v. 25%) and less likely to be in touch with other carers (49% v. 71%). They received on average less by way of pay and allowances than other foster carers. This, however, was mainly because they were much less likely to receive a relatively high rate. On average they were less satisfied with fostering, with only 29 per cent saying that they obtained a lot of satisfaction from it as opposed to 47 per cent of the other carers.

Overall our findings suggested that kinship carers were a diverse group. Some saw themselves essentially as kin and therefore in no need of training. Others felt a need for training and were resentful that they did not get it. We ourselves concluded that training should be provided for those who wanted it, and that their rather distinctive needs for support should be recognised. They have, for example, particular issues in their relationship with birth families. Their material disadvantages mean that practical support may be particularly relevant. The lack of differences between relatives and others in terms of age and ethnicity (a contrast with findings from the USA) also suggested that there might be scope for recruiting grandmothers and relative carers from minority ethnic groups.

References

Adamson, G. (1973) *The Caretakers.* London: Bookstall Publications.

Aldgate, J. and Hawley, D. (1986) *Foster Home Breakdown.* London: British Agencies for Adoption and Fostering.

Aldgate, J., Heath, A., Colton, M. and Simms, M. (1993) 'Social work and the education of children in foster care.' *Adoption and Fostering 17,* 3, 25–34.

Ames Reed, J. (1993) *We Have Learned a Lot from Them: Foster care for young people with learning difficulties.* London: National Children's Bureau/ Barnado's.

Baxter, S. (1989) *Fostering Breakdown: An Internal Study.* Belfast: Department of Health and Social Security (Northern Ireland).

Bebbington, A. and Miles, J. (1990) 'The supply of foster families for children in care.' *British Journal of Social Work 20,* 4, 283–307.

Berridge, D. (1997) *Foster Care: A Research Review.* London: The Stationery Office.

Berridge, D. and Cleaver, H. (1987) *Foster Home Breakdown.* Oxford: Blackwell.

Bowling, A. (1991) *Measuring Health: A Review of Quality of Life Measurement Scales.* Buckingham: Open University Press.

Broad, B. (1999) 'Kinship care: enabling and supporting child placements with relatives and friends.' In British Agencies for Adoption and Fostering (ed) *Assessment, Preparation and Support.* London: British Agencies for Adoption and Fostering.

Broad, B. (ed) (2001a) *Kinship Care: The Placement Choice for Children and Young People.* Lyme Regis: Russell House Publishing.

Broad, B. (2001b) 'Kinship placements: supporting children in placements with extended family and friends.' *Adoption and Fostering 25,* 2, 33–41.

Caesar, G., Parchment, M. and Berridge, D. (1994) *Black Perspectives on Services for Children in Need.* Barkingside: Barnado's and National Children's Bureau.

Calder, M. (1999) 'Managing allegations of abuse against carers.' In A. Wheal (ed) *Companion to Foster Care.* London: Russell House Publishing.

Chamberlain, P. (1998) *Blueprints for Violence Prevention; Book 8 Multidimensional Treatment Foster Care.* Colorado: University of Colorado, Centre for Study and Prevention of Violence.

Clark, H., Prange, M., Lee, B., Boyd, L., McDonald, B. and Stewart, E. (1994) 'Improving adjustment outcomes for foster children with emotional and behavioural disorders: early findings from a controlled study on individualised services.' *Journal of Emotional and Behavioural Disorders 2,* 207–218.

Cleaver, H. (2000) *Fostering Family Contact.* London: The Stationery Office.

Coffin, G. (1993) *Changing Child Care: The Children Act 1989 and the Management of Change.* London: National Children's Bureau.

Dando, I. and Minty, B. (1987) 'What makes good foster parents?' *British Journal of Social Work 17*, 383–400.

Department of Health (1991a) *The Children Act 1989. Guidance and Regulations: Volume 3 – Family Placements.* London: HMSO.

Department of Health (1991b) *Working Together Under the Children Act 1989: A Guide to Arrangements for Inter Agency Co-operation for the Protection of Children Against Abuse.* London: HMSO.

Department of Health (1999) *Children Looked After by Local Authorities: Year Ending March 1998.* London: Government Statistical Service.

Department of Health (2000) *Prime Minister's Review: Adoption.* London: Department of Health, Performance and Innovation Unit.

Department of Health (2003) *Children Looked After by Local Authorities: Year Ending March 2002.* London: Government Statistical Service.

Farmer, E., Moyers, S. and Lipscombe, J. (2002) *Children Placed with Relatives or Family.* Report to the Department of Health. Bristol: University of Bristol.

Fisher, T., Gibbs, I., Sinclair, I. and Wilson, K. (2000) 'Sharing the care: the qualities sought of social workers by foster carers.' *Child and Family Social Work 5*, 225–233.

Garnett, L. (1992) *Leaving Care and After.* London: National Children's Bureau.

George V. (1970) *Foster Care: Theory and Practice.* London: Routledge and Kegan Paul.

Goldberg, D. and Williams, P. (1988) *A User's Guide to the General Health Questionnaire.* Windsor: National Foundation for Educational Research.

Gorin, S. (1997) *Time to Listen? Views and Experiences of Family Placement.* Portsmouth: Social Services Research and Information Unit, Portsmouth University.

Gray, P. and Parr, E. (1957) *Children in Care and the Recruitment of Foster Parents.* London: Home Office.

Hazel, N. (1981) *A Bridge to Independence.* Oxford: Basil Blackwell.

Heath, A., Colton, M. and Aldgate, J. (1994) 'Failure to escape: a longitudinal study of foster children's educational attainment.' *British Journal of Social Work 19*, 6, 447–460.

Hicks, C. and Nixon, S. (1989) 'Allegations of child abuse: foster carers as victims.' *Foster Care 58*, 14–15.

Hicks, C. and Nixon, S. (1991) 'Unfounded allegations of child abuse in the UK: a survey of foster parents' reactions to investigative procedures.' *Children and Youth Services Review 15*, 2, 249–260.

Hill, M., Nutter, R., Giltinan, D., Hudson, J. and Galway, B. (1999) 'A comparative survey of specialist fostering in the UK and North America.' In M. Hill (ed) *Signposts in Fostering: Policy, Practice and Research Issues.* London: British Agencies for Adoption and Fostering, London.

House of Commons Health Committee (1998) *Children Looked After by Local Authorities.* London: HMSO.

Jackson, S. (1994) 'Educating children in residential and foster care.' *Oxford Review of Education 20*, 3, 267–279.

Jackson, S. (ed) (2001) *Nobody Ever Told Us School Mattered.* London: British Agencies for Adoption and Fostering.

Jones, E. (1975) 'A study of those who cease to foster.' *British Journal of Social Work 5*, 1, 31–41.

Kaplan, C. (1998) 'The biological children of foster parents in the foster family.' *Child and Adolescent Social Work 5*, 4, 281–289.

Kirton, D. (2001) 'Love and money: payment and the fostering task.' *Child and Family Social Work 6*, 199–208.

Leat, D. (1990) *For Love and Money: The Role of Payment in Encouraging the Provision of Care.* York: Joseph Rowntree Foundation.

Moralee, S. (1999) *An Investigation into the Determinants of the Supply of Foster Care in England at Local Authority Level.* MSc Health Economics, University of York.

National Foster Care Association (1997) *Foster Care in Crisis.* London: National Foster Care Association.

Oldfield, N. (1997) *The Adequacy of Foster Care Allowances.* Aldershot: Ashgate.

Packman, J. and Hall, C. (1998) *From Care to Accommodation: the Implementation of Section 20 of the Children Act 1989.* London: Stationery Office.

Parker, R. (1978) 'Foster care in context.' *Adoption and Fostering 2*, 27–32.

Part, D. (1993) 'Fostering as seen by the carers' children.' *Adoption and Fostering 17*, 1, 26–31.

Pithouse, A. and Parry, O. (1999) 'Local authority fostering in Wales: The All Wales Review.' In M. Hill (ed) *Signposts in Fostering: Policy, Practice and Research Issues.* London: British Agencies for Adoption and Fostering.

Pugh, G. (1996) 'Seen but not heard? Addressing the needs of children who foster.' *Adoption and Fostering 20*, 1, 3–41.

Quinton, D., Rushton, A., Dance, C. and Mayes, D. (1998) *Joining New Families – A Study of Adoption and Fostering in Middle Childhood.* Chichester: John Wiley.

Ramsay, D. (1996) 'Recruiting and retaining foster carers: implications of a professional service in Fife.' *Adoption and Fostering 20*, 1, 42–46.

Reindfleisch, N., Bean, G. and Denby, R. (1998) 'Why foster parents continue and cease to foster.' *Journal of Sociology and Social Welfare 25*, 1, 5–24.

Rhodes, K., Orme, J. and Buehler, C. (2001) 'A comparison of foster parents who quit consider quitting and plan to continue fostering.' *Social Services Review 75*, 1, 84–115.

Rowe, J., Cain, H., Hundleby, M. and Keane, A. (1984) *Long Term Foster Care.* London: Batsford.

Rowe, J., Hundleby, M. and Garnett, L. (1989) *Child Care Now.* London: British Agencies for Adoption and Fostering.

Sellick, C. (1992) *Supporting Short-Term Foster Carers.* Aldershot: Avebury.

Sellick, C. (2002) 'The aims and principles of independent fostering agencies: a view from the inside.' *Adoption and Fostering 26*, 1, 56–63.

Sellick, C. and Thoburn, J. (1996) *What Works in Family Placement?* Ilford: Barnado's.

Shaw, M. and Hipgrave, A. (1983) *Specialist Fostering.* London: Batsford.

Shaw, M. and Hipgrave, T. (1989) 'Specialist fostering 1988 – a research study.' *Adoption and Fostering 13*, 3, 17–21.

Simon, J. (1975) 'The effect of foster care payment levels on the number of children given homes.' *Social Services Review 49*, 405–411.

Soothill, K. and Derbyshire, M. (1982) 'Retention of foster parents.' *Adoption and Fostering 6*, 38–43.

Stein, M. (1997) *What Works in Leaving Care.* Barkingside: Barnado's.

Sykes, J., Sinclair, I., Gibbs, I. and Wilson, K. (2002) 'Kinship and stranger foster care: how do they compare?' *Adoption and Fostering 26*, 2, 38–48.

Thoburn, J. (1996) 'Psychological parenting and child placement.' In D. Howe (ed) *Attachment and Loss in Child and Family Social Work.* Aldershot: Avebury.

Thoburn, J., Murdoch, A. and O'Brien, A. (1986) *Permanence in Child Care.* Oxford: Blackwell.

Thoburn, J., Norford L. and Rashid, S. (2000) *Permanent Family Placement for Children of Minority Ethnic Origin.* London: Jessica Kingsley Publishers.

Triseliotis, J., Borland, M. and Hill, M. (2000) *Delivering Foster Care.* London: British Agencies for Adoption and Fostering.

Utting, W. (1997) *People Like Us: Report of the Review of Safeguards for Children Living Away from Home.* London: Department of Health and Welsh Office.

Walker, M., Hill, M. and Triseliotis, J. (2002) *Testing the Limits of Foster Care: Fostering as an Alternative to Secure Accommodation.* London: British Association of Adoption and Fostering.

Waterhouse, S. (1997) *The Organisation of Fostering Services: A Study of the Arrangements for Delivery of Fostering Services in England.* London: National Foster Care Association.

Waterhouse, S. and Brocklesbury, E. (1999) *Placement Choices for Children in Temporary Foster Care.* London: National Foster Care Association.

Wheal, A. (1995) *The Foster Carers' Handbook.* London: National Foster Care Association.

Wheal, A. (1999) 'Family and friends who are carers.' In A. Wheal (ed) *Companion to Foster Care.* London: Russell House Publishing.

Wilson, K., Sinclair, I. and Gibbs, I. (2000) 'The trouble with foster care: the impact of stressful events on foster carers.' *British Journal of Social Work 30*, 193–209.

Subject Index

abused children 53, 96
adoption 41, 68, 158
adults in the family 24
age differences, birth/foster children
   relationship with outcome measures 80,
     82–3
   unrelated to leaving/staying 132
age of carers
   and difficulties in attending training 110
   General Questionnaire results 23–4
   relationship with leaving/staying 129
   relationship with outcome measures 75–6
age of foster children
   and carers' appraisal of out-of-hours service
     118–19
   and difficulties in attending training 110
   General Questionnaire results 35–6
   and income from fostering 121
   and kind of fostering 39
   and likelihood of carers working 21
   and likelihood of stressful 'events' 93, 104n
   relationship with leaving/staying 132, 151,
     152
   relationship with outcome measures 79,
     81–2
agencies 33–4
allegations 88, 103, 167
   carers' appraisal of local authority
     arrangements 118
   and intention to leave 102
   meaning for carers 94–5
   proportion of carers reporting 91
   and symptoms of strain 100
allowances *see* financial support
America/USA
   foster care adoptions 158
   fostering studies 12, 164
   special schemes, theoretical justification 9
   therapeutic fostering models 159
approvals 37–9
   carer vs. social workers views of status 37
   placements, preference and 43–4
   variation between authorities 39, 40, 155
'arm twisting' 41, 99

birth parents
   changing relationships with 9, 89

difficulties with 95–6, 103–4
   and intention to leave 102
   proportion of carers reporting 90, 91
   and symptoms of strain 100
birth children
   effect of foster children's difficult behaviour
     53–4
   loss issues 54
   needs 51–2
   overall impact of fostering on 55–6
   support from 50–1, 56
black carers *see* minority ethnic carers
black children *see* minority ethnic children
Britain/United Kingdom
   fostering studies 12, 18–19, 115
   lack of coherent policy 10

carers groups *see* fostering groups
census 13–14
   and calculation of leaving rates 126–8
   pro-forma sample 177–8
   sample representativeness 174–5
   social characteristics of carers 19–23
characteristics of carers and families 161
   and attitudes to payment 27–9
   census results 19–23
   General Questionnaire results 23–9
   recent research 11–12
   relationship with outcome measures 75–9
     multivariate analysis 148–52
   relationship with leaving/staying 129–31,
     141
Child and Family Social Work 108
Children Act (1989) 9, 38, 89, 90
child's social workers 33
   support from 115–17
   unrelated to leaving/staying 137
Choice Protects 10
commitment to fostering 83, 155
   commitment to individuals vs. commitment
     in general 131–2, 142
   relationship to leaving/staying 139–40
community care 41
'conditions of service' 61–2

difficult behaviour
   and financial support 121
   impact on family life 53–4, 89, 96, 156
   impact on well-being 67–8
disabled children 37, 39, 159

Author Index

Sellick, C. 10, 11, 12, 33, 88, 157, 163
Shaw, M. 9, 38
Simon, J. 164
Sinclair, I. 104n
Soothill, K. 75
Stein, M. 10
Sykes, J. 97, 158, 179

Thoburn, J. 88, 89, 115, 157
Triseliotis, J. 9, 10, 11, 12, 14, 18, 21, 24, 25,
    26, 27, 29, 30, 31n, 32, 33–4, 35, 36,
    44,
46, 56, 83, 88, 89, 99, 109, 110, 113, 115,
    117, 118, 124, 127, 128, 129, 131,
    141, 154, 155, 157, 161, 163, 164,
    172n,

Utting, W. 8

Walker, M. 13, 115, 160, 170
Waterhouse, S. 10, 12, 18, 19, 24, 33, 37, 39,
    127, 155, 164
Wheal, A. 88, 158
Williams, P. 86n
Wilson, K. 104n